Seasoning the Fox Valley

Recipes Edited and Adapted by
Carleen Bart, Carol Bushnell, and Penny Newkirk

Illustrated by Sandy Kubinski
Cover Watercolor by Carleen Bart

**All proceeds from the sale of this cookbook benefit the
PADS® Ministry at Hesed House**

For more information contact: Hesed House
659 South River Street
Aurora, Illinois 60506

Copyright © 1996 Public Action to Deliver Shelter, Inc.®

All rights reserved. Reproduction in whole or in part of any portion in any form without permission is prohibited.

First Edition

ISBN: 0-942495-57-8

Library of Congress Catalog Card Number: 96-68053

Published by
Public Action to Deliver Shelter, Inc.®
659 South River Street
Aurora, IL 60506

Printed by
Palmer Publications, Inc.
PO Box 296
Amherst, WI 54406

Printed on recycled paper

*This book is dedicated to the homeless of the Fox Valley
and to the volunteers who give them hope at Hesed House.*

Special Thanks to:

S Rose Marie Lorentzen, BVM, Hesed House Executive Director
Diane Nilan, Hesed House PADS Coordinator

Carleen Bart, Cover Watercolor
Sandy Kubinski, Illustrations
Mary Ann Schwieger, Hesed House Drawing

The Friends of PADS who shared their favorite family recipes.

Our friends who helped us test and taste each recipe:
Vel Ball, Paula Brewer, Mary Jo Cessna, Carol Erickson,
Marilyn Hendry, and Allison Rainboth

The person who made our cookbook professional and consistent:
Mary Lou Conley, Proofreading and Editing

Our families, our main support and best tasters:
Bill, Brad, Dave, Eric, Jeff, Joe, Justin, Mark and Randy

We cooked, ate, learned and laughed together. We gave and yet received so much more—friendship, shared experiences and treasured memories.

Carleen Bart
Carol Bushnell
Penny Newkirk

*"To everything there is a season,
and a time to every purpose under heaven..."*

Ecclesiastes 3 : 1

Friends and Contributors

Myrtle Abelt
Goldie Anderson
Suyapa Anderson
Donna Andrini
Vel Ball
Carleen Bart
Eric Bart
Fern Bart
Justin Bart
Kerry Bart-Raber
Kathy Blomquist
Joan C. Boeman
Nola Boyd
Paula Brewer
Jane Briner
Maggie Burmeister
Marge Burr
Carol Bushnell
Jo Cessna
Carole Clark
Margaret Clark
Peggy Collyer
Mary Lou Conley
Joanne Cooke, M.S., R.D.
Joyce Currie
Barbara Day
Sally DeCardy
Susan Deuchler
Nancy DiMaio
Patty Dritsas
Carol Erickson
Ron and Jackie Gall
Martha Gimnig
Karen Gimse
Dorothy Gunter
Fran Gustafson
Jeane Hagerty
Sarah Hampton
Betty Hanley
Marilyn Hendry

Lisa Herrera
Eleanor Hoffman
Barbara Holmes
Linda Howells
Virginia Hudson
Carol Hundley
Marjorie Johnson
Carol Juntunen
Margaret Kalte
Margaret Kelly
Gisela Kinscheck
Pat Kitner
Jan F. Kohl
John Kohl
Susan Kreager
Sandy Kubinski
Judy Legat
Pam Lose
Mi Loran
Mickey Lubcke
Carol Ludemann
LaVerne Maher
Sue Mahood
Mary and Michael Marks
Mary Jane McFee
Jean McPartlin
Julia and Ken McPartlin
Julie McPartlin
Marlene McPartlin
Marge Mennerick
Sharon Mennerick
Julie Meredith
Gladys Metcalf
Elizabeth Michaelsen
Emma Michels
Mary Lou Miller
Tom & Dorothy Milnamow
Roberta Mitchell
Barb Mitchinson

Terese Moore
Grainne Murphy
Penny Newkirk
Olga Newkirk
Anne Nordstrom
Nancy Norgaard
Laverne Northway
Patricia Novak
Donna Nowatzki
Colleen O'Neil
Marla Olson
Diane Olsen
Lois Park, R.D.
Sue Peterson
Jay and Kelly Phelps
Carlleen Pierson
Marilyn Przwara
Allison Rainboth
Billye Renwick
Martha Rioux
Mary Ann Schweiger
James Simmers
Carol Smith
Roberta Sprowl
Mary Stasek
Ronald Stazak
Judy Stratman
Margaret Taylor
Barbara Taff
Sue Taylor
Amy Thompson
Ed Troy
S Joanne Vallero, CSJ
Adrian Walters
John & Mark Weaver
Mary Jo Weddle
Barb Wiebmer
Linda Wirtz
Shirley Yuill

Friends and Contributors

Carvers on the Lake Restaurant and Inn
N5529 County Road A
Green Lake, WI 54941

Color and Beyond Inc.
336 Gundersen Drive
Carol Stream, IL 60188

Congregational United Church of Christ
214 Walnut Street
St. Charles, IL 60174

Cooking Craft
1415 W. Main Street
St. Charles, IL 60174

DuPage Korean United Methodist Church
21 E. Franklin Street
Naperville, IL 60540

Elgin High School Clumsy Chef Student Restaurant
1200 Maroon Drive
Elgin, IL 60120

Garfield Farm Museum
3N 016 Garfield Road
P.O. Box 403
LaFox, IL 60147

Grace United Methodist Church
300 E. Gartner Road
Naperville, IL 60540

Hill Street Bed and Breakfast
353 W. Hill Street
Spring Green, WI 53588

Inglenook Pantry
11 N. 5th Street
Geneva, IL 60134

Just Ask Jo Catering
1387 Prosser Drive
Sycamore, IL 60178

Kwik Kopy Printing
105 S. 14th Street
St. Charles, IL 60174

Persimmon Tree
127 S. Third Street
Geneva, IL 60134

Pine-Apple Orchard
01N 145 Watson Road
Maple Park, IL 60151

Valley Shopping Center Merchants Association
1400 W. Main Street
St. Charles, IL 60174

Thank You!

Ministries at Hesed House

The unique model of religious and civic cooperation found at Hesed House makes it possible for persons who are physically, emotionally, or mentally handicapped or those in economic crisis to receive food, clothing, shelter and, most importantly, a chance to hope again.

PADS' Ministries include:

- PADS Emergency Shelter, which offers a warm, safe place to stay for an average of 120 homeless adults and children each night during winter months;

- PADS A.M. (And More!) Drop-in Center, which extends hospitality and assistance to an average of 95 PADS guests during daytime hours;

- Transitional Living Community, a temporary residence for up to 50 homeless families and individuals while they overcome the causes of their homelessness;

- Advocacy, which involves volunteers in efforts to alleviate root causes of poverty and homelessness.

Other Hesed House Ministries:

- Aurora Soup Kitchen, which serves a hot, nutritious noon meal to hundreds of low income/homeless persons;

- Interfaith Food Pantry, which provides groceries to 12,000+ people each month;

- Clothes Closet, which distributes "gently-used" clothing to families and individuals without charge.

Since 1985, when Hesed House first opened, these ministries have received wide-spread support from area faith communities, individuals, businesses, and organizations in addition to receiving government grants (which are dwindling). Over 94¢ of every dollar received goes for direct assistance. The PADS ministry at Hesed House depends upon the generosity of the Fox Valley community for support.

Spring

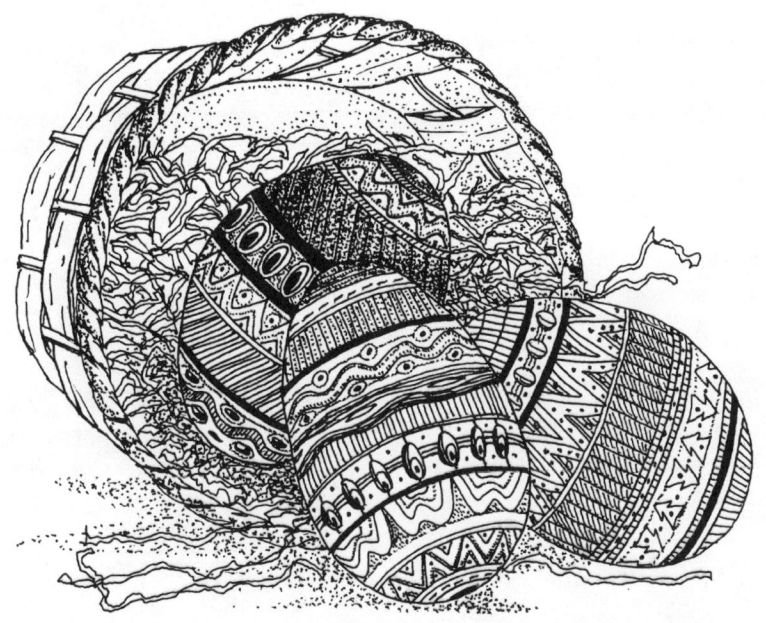

Table of Contents

Brunch
Breads for Brunch
Appetizers
Soups
Salads
Side Dishes
Entrees
Desserts

Spring Brunch

VEGETABLE FRITTATA

3/4 cup green pepper, chopped	1/4 cup half-and-half
1 1/2 cups fresh mushrooms, sliced	2 (8 oz.) packages cream cheese, cubed
1 1/2 cups zucchini, chopped	1 1/2 cups Cheddar cheese, shredded
3/4 cup onion, chopped	2 cups day-old bread, crusts removed and cubed
1 large clove garlic, minced	1 teaspoon salt
3 tablespoons vegetable oil	1/4 teaspoon pepper
6 eggs, beaten	

1. Saute green pepper, mushrooms, zucchini and onion in oil. Add garlic and cook until vegetables are tender. Cool slightly.

2. Beat eggs with half-and-half. Add cream cheese, Cheddar, bread, salt and pepper.

3. Preheat oven to 350°.

4. Combine vegetable mixture with egg mixture. Pour into a well-greased 10-inch springform pan. Bake in preheated oven for 1 hour or until set in center. Cool 10 minutes and remove springform rim. Cut into wedges and serve.

Serves 8   *Penny Newkirk*

SAUSAGE STRATA

2 pounds pork sausage, fried and drained
4 cups milk
12 beaten eggs
12 slices white bread, crusts removed and cubed
1 teaspoon dry mustard
2 1/2 cups sharp Cheddar cheese, grated
salt and pepper to taste

1. Grease 10 x 15-inch or 9 x 13-inch pan. Sprinkle bread in pan. Add sausage and cheese on top of bread. In a separate bowl, mix eggs, milk, salt, pepper and mustard. Pour over bread and sausage. Cover and refrigerate overnight.

2. Preheat oven to 350°. Bake for 1 hour. Let stand 15 minutes before serving.

Serves 12   *Carol Erickson*

Spring Brunch

SHRIMP BRUNCH CASSEROLE

6 eggs, hard-boiled	4 tablespoons flour
2 tablespoons mayonnaise	1/2 teaspoon salt
1/4 teaspoon dry mustard	3 cups milk
1/4 teaspoon salt	1/4 cup Cheddar cheese, grated
freshly ground pepper	1 cup seasoned bread crumbs
2 cups fresh shrimp, cooked and deveined	2 tablespoons butter, melted paprika
3 tablespoons butter	parsley

1. Preheat oven to 350°.

2. Devil eggs with mayonnaise, mustard, salt and pepper. Place in greased 7 x 11-inch baking dish with the shrimp.

3. Melt butter. Add flour and salt. Blend well. Add milk gradually, stirring until blended. Cook, stirring constantly until slightly thickened. Add cheese. Cook until melted.

4. Pour sauce over eggs and shrimp. Top with seasoned bread crumbs mixed with melted butter. Bake for 35 minutes. Garnish with paprika and parsley.

Serves 6 — *Carol Bushnell*

CHEESE BLINTZES

1 giant loaf white bread	3/4 cup sugar, divided
2 (8 oz.) packages cream cheese, room temperature	1 cup butter or margarine
2 egg yolks	1/4 teaspoon ground cinnamon

1. For filling: Combine cream cheese, egg yolks and 1/2 cup sugar. Mix well.

2. For coating: Melt butter, 1/4 cup sugar and cinnamon. Keep warm.

3. Cut off bread crusts. Flatten each slice of bread with rolling pin until very thin. Spread each slice with filling. Roll up jelly roll fashion. Dip into coating mixture.

4. Chill on waxed paper.

5. Preheat oven to 350°. Bake 15-20 minutes. Serve warm.

Makes 35-40 pieces — *Paula Brewer*

Spring Brunch

RANCHERO EGG CASSEROLE

6 tablespoons margarine, divided	1/2 cup green onion, chopped
2 tablespoons flour	1/4 cup green pepper, chopped
dash pepper	1/4 cup red pepper, chopped
2 cups milk	2 tablespoons fresh cilantro, chopped
1 cup co-jack cheese, shredded	12 eggs, beaten
1 stick (4 oz.) chorizo sausage	1 1/2 cups cornflakes, crushed

1. In a saucepan melt 2 tablespoons margarine. Add flour and pepper. Cook 1-2 minutes until bubbly. Add milk and cook until thickened. Add cheese and remove from heat.

2. In a skillet cook sausage. Remove from skillet. Add onion and peppers and saute until tender. Return sausage to pan. Add eggs and cilantro. Scramble egg mixture, but still retain moisture.

3. Grease an 11 x 7-inch baking dish. Combine cheese mixture with egg mixture and blend lightly. Add to prepared pan. (May be made to this point and refrigerated overnight.)

4. Preheat oven to 350°.

5. Melt remaining 4 tablespoons margarine and combine with crushed cornflakes. Sprinkle on top. Bake uncovered 30-35 minutes or until golden brown.

Serves 8-10 — *Penny Newkirk*

KUGEL WITH APPLESAUCE

8 ounces wide egg noodles, cooked and drained	2 eggs
1 cup butter	2 cups cornflakes, crushed
2 cups milk	1/4 cup sugar
1 (24-28 oz.) jar unsweetened applesauce	1 1/2 teaspoons ground cinnamon
1 (8 oz.) package cream cheese, room temperature	1/2 cup raisins, optional

1. Preheat oven to 350°.

2. Melt butter. Add milk. Do not boil.

3. Beat cream cheese and eggs. Add applesauce, butter and milk mixture, noodles and raisins. Stir with spoon until blended.

4. Pour into greased 9 x 13-inch pan. Sprinkle with cornflakes.

5. Mix cinnamon and sugar. Sprinkle over cornflakes.

6. Bake 60 minutes. Cool slightly, but serve warm.

Serves 12-16 — *Colleen O'Neil*

Spring Brunch

FRENCH TOAST FOR BRUNCH

12 eggs, beaten	1/2 cup maple syrup
2 cups milk	12-14 slices day-old bread, crusts removed, cubed and divided
2 (8 oz.) packages cream cheese, cubed	2-3 tablespoons cinnamon sugar mixture

1. Place half of the bread on the bottom of greased 9 x 13-inch baking dish.
2. Layer cream cheese and remaining bread.
3. Mix eggs, milk and syrup. Pour over bread and cheese mixture. Sprinkle cinnamon sugar on top. Refrigerate overnight.
4. Preheat oven to 375°. Bake 50-60 minutes or until knife inserted in center comes out clean. Serve with warm syrup.

Serves 10-12   *Barb Wiebmer*

Note: Add sliced apples and raisins for a fruited variety. Also see Fruited Pancake Syrups (See Recipes).

HOT CHICKEN SALAD

4 cups chicken, cooked and cubed	1 tablespoon onion, finely chopped
3/4 cup mayonnaise	2 pimentos, chopped
3/4 cup condensed cream of chicken soup	1 cup Cheddar cheese, grated
2 tablespoons lemon juice	1 1/2 cups potato chips, crushed
2 cups celery, chopped	2/3 cup almonds, toasted and chopped
4 hard-cooked eggs, chopped	

1. Combine mayonnaise, cream of chicken soup and lemon juice. Add chicken, celery, eggs, onion and pimento.
2. Place in greased 9 x 13-inch baking dish. Top with cheese, potato chips and almonds. Cover and refrigerate overnight.
3. Preheat oven to 400°.
4. Bake uncovered 20-25 minutes.

Serves 8   *Barb Mitchinson*

Spring Brunch

SPICED BLUEBERRY JAM

3 pints fresh blueberries (crushed to make 4 cups)
2 tablespoons lemon juice
1 box Sure-Jell
4 cups sugar
1/2 teaspoon ground cloves
1/2 teaspoon ground cinnamon
1/2 teaspoon ground allspice

1. Measure sugar and spices into a bowl.

2. Mix Sure-Jell with fruit and lemon juice in large saucepan. Cook over high heat until mixture comes to a full rolling boil, stirring constantly.

3. Stir in sugar and spices all at once. Return to a full rolling boil. Boil 1 minute, stirring constantly.

4. Remove pan from heat. Skim off foam with metal spoon. Then stir and skim by turns for 5 minutes to slightly cool and prevent fruit from floating.

5. Ladle quickly into sterilized jars, leaving one 1/2-inch space at top. Wipe jar rims. Cover quickly with flat lids. Screw bands tightly.

6. Seal at once by submerging jars in boiling water, 1 inch over top of jar. Boil for 10 minutes. Remove from water. Cool. Make sure lids are sealed by pressing on center of lid. Center should be firm and not spring back.

Makes 6 cups *Paula Brewer*

Spring Brunch

BELGIAN MALTED WAFFLES

2 cups all-purpose flour	1 teaspoon vanilla
1 tablespoon baking powder	4 eggs, separated
1/2 teaspoon salt	1/2 cup vegetable oil
1 tablespoon sugar	1 3/4 cups milk
2 tablespoons vanilla malted milk powder	

1. Preheat greased Belgian waffle iron.
2. Combine flour, baking powder, salt, sugar and malted milk powder.
3. In a separate bowl, beat egg yolks until thick and lemon colored. Add vanilla, vegetable oil and milk. Stir into flour mixture until smooth, but do not overbeat.
4. Beat egg whites until peaked but not dry. Fold gently into batter.
5. Bake waffles using Belgian waffle iron instructions.

Makes 4-5 waffles *Carleen Bart*

PUMPKIN WAFFLES

1/4 cup butter, melted	1 teaspoon ground cinnamon
1 1/2 cups flour	3 eggs, separated
1 tablespoon baking powder	1 cup milk
1/2 teaspoon salt	1 cup cooked or canned pumpkin
1/4 teaspoon ground nutmeg	

1. Preheat greased waffle iron.
2. Combine flour, baking powder, salt, nutmeg and cinnamon.
3. Beat egg yolks, then combine with milk, pumpkin and butter. Stir in dry ingredients.
4. Beat egg whites until they form soft peaks. Fold into batter.
5. Bake waffles using waffle iron instructions.

Makes 4 waffles *Justin Bart*

Note: Wonderful served with Cinnamon Syrup (See Recipe).

Spring Brunch

CINNAMON SYRUP

   1   cup sugar
1/2   cup light corn syrup
1/4   cup water
1/2   teaspoon ground cinnamon
1/2   cup whipping cream or evaporated milk

1. In small saucepan, stir together sugar, corn syrup, water and cinnamon. Stirring constantly, bring to a boil over moderate heat. Boil 2 minutes. Remove from heat. Stir in cream.

2. Cool at least 30 minutes. Syrup will thicken as it cools. Will keep in refrigerator for several months. Serve warm or at room temperature.

Makes 1 1/3 cups   *Judy Legat*

BLUEBERRY SYRUP

1/2   cup sugar
  1   tablespoon cornstarch
1/4   cup water
1/4   cup light corn syrup
  2   teaspoons lemon juice
  2   cups fresh blueberries

1. Combine sugar and cornstarch in 1-quart micro-proof casserole. Add water, syrup and lemon juice. Stir in blueberries.

2. Microwave on full power for 4 1/2-5 minutes, or until thickened. For thicker syrup, add 1 more teaspoon of cornstarch.

Makes 1 3/4 cups   *Judy Legat*

*Spring
Brunch*

FRESH STRAWBERRY SYRUP

*1 pint fresh strawberries,
    hulled, halved and slightly mashed
1 cup sugar
3/4 cup light corn syrup*

1. Place strawberries in a 3-quart saucepan. Cook over medium heat, stirring occasionally, until strawberries come to a full boil (6-8 minutes).

2. Line strainer with cheesecloth and place over large bowl. Pour hot strawberries into strainer, mashing with back of spoon to extract juice. Discard pulp.

3. Return juice to pan and add sugar and corn syrup. Cook over medium heat until mixture comes to a full boil (9-10 minutes). Boil 1 minute. With large metal spoon skim foam from top. Store refrigerated.

4. One (16 oz.) bag frozen strawberries may be substituted for 1 pint fresh strawberries. Increase cooking time of strawberries to 15 minutes.

Makes 2 cups *Judy Legat*

*Note: The St. Charles Congregational United Church of Christ has been hosting
    Labor Day pancake breakfasts since 1953. These syrups have been a favorite.*

Spring Breads

BAVARIAN APPLE TORTE

Crust:
- 1/2 cup margarine, softened
- 1/3 cup sugar
- 1/4 teaspoon vanilla
- 1 cup flour

Cheese filling:
- 1 (8 oz.) package cream cheese, softened
- 1/4 cup sugar
- 1 egg
- 1 teaspoon vanilla

Topping:
- 1/3 cup sugar
- 1/2 teaspoon ground cinnamon
- 4 cups apples, peeled and sliced
- 1/4 cup slivered almonds

1. Preheat oven to 450°.

2. Prepare crust: Cream margarine and sugar. Add flour and vanilla. Mix well.

3. Grease bottom and sides of a 9-inch springform pan. Spread crust on bottom.

4. Prepare filling: Blend cream cheese and sugar until smooth. Add egg and vanilla. Pour on top of prepared crust.

5. Prepare topping: Mix cinnamon and sugar. Toss with apples. Spoon apple mixture over cream cheese layer and top with slivered almonds.

6. Bake for 10 minutes. Reduce heat to 400° and continue baking for 25 minutes. Cool on rack before releasing springform.

Serves 8   *Margaret Clark*

Spring Breads

BANANA PECAN BREAD

2	cups butter	1/2	teaspoon salt
1	cup sugar	1	teaspoon baking soda
3	eggs, beaten	1	tablespoon water
2	cups flour	4	large very ripe bananas, mashed
1/2	teaspoon baking powder	1	cup pecans, chopped

1. Preheat oven to 350°. Grease 1 loaf pan.

2. Cream butter and sugar until light and fluffy. Add eggs.

3. Combine flour, baking powder and salt. Add to creamed mixture.

4. Dissolve baking soda in water and mix with bananas. Stir into the batter. Add pecans.

5. Place batter into greased pan. Bake for 60 minutes, or until toothpick inserted into center comes out clean.

Makes 1 loaf *Carol Bushnell*

STRAWBERRY BREAD

3	cups flour	1	cup vegetable oil
2	cups sugar	4	eggs
1	teaspoon salt	2	(10 oz.) packages frozen
1	teaspoon baking powder		strawberries, thawed
1	teaspoon cinnamon	1	(8 oz.) package cream cheese, softened

1. Preheat oven to 350°.

2. Drain and chop strawberries, reserving 1/2 cup juice.

3. Combine flour, sugar, salt, baking powder and cinnamon. In a separate bowl combine vegetable oil, eggs and strawberries.

4. Stir liquids into dry ingredients just until blended.

5. Pour into 2 greased loaf pans. Bake 50-60 minutes or until toothpick inserted in center comes out clean. Remove from pans. Cool on rack.

6. Strawberry Spread: Blend 1/2 cup reserved strawberry juice with cream cheese.

Makes 2 loaves *Gladys Metcalf*
Barbara Holmes

Spring Breads

CAPPUCCINO CHIP MUFFINS

   2   *cups all-purpose flour*
 1/2 *cup sugar*
2 1/2 *teaspoons baking powder*
   3   *tablespoons powdered instant coffee*
 1/2 *teaspoon salt*
   1   *cup milk*
 1/2 *cup butter, melted*
   1   *egg, beaten*
   1   *teaspoon vanilla*
 1/2 *cup mini chocolate chips*

1. Preheat oven to 375°. Grease 48 mini-muffin pans.

2. In a large bowl mix together flour, sugar, baking powder, instant coffee and salt.

3. In a separate bowl whisk together milk, butter, egg, and vanilla. Add to dry ingredients. Stir just to combine. Add mini chocolate chips. Spoon into mini-muffin pans until two-thirds full. Bake 15 minutes. Cool 5 minutes. Remove from pans.

Makes 48 mini-muffins   *Kelly and Jay Phelps*
                                                                                 the Hill Street Bed and Breakfast

Spring Breads

SWEET NUT BRAID COFFEE CAKE

2	packages dry yeast	*Filling:*	
1/2	cup water (110°)	1/4	cup butter or margarine
1/3	cup butter, melted	1 1/2	cups powdered sugar
1/3	cup sugar	3 1/2	teaspoons milk
2 1/2	teaspoons salt	1	teaspoon vanilla
1	cup milk (110°)	1/4	teaspoon ground nutmeg
2	eggs	1	cup nuts, chopped and divided
5-5 1/2	cups unsifted flour	1	egg white
1	teaspoon ground cardamom	1	tablespoon water
1	tablespoon lemon rind, grated		

1. Dissolve yeast in warm water. Add butter, salt, sugar and milk.

2. Stir in lemon rind, cardamom and eggs. Gradually add enough flour to form a soft dough. Knead on floured surface until smooth, adding flour only as needed to avoid sticking. Place in greased bowl and turn over to grease top. Cover and let rise until double in size (about 1 1/2 hours).

3. For filling: Cream butter. Add powdered sugar, milk, nutmeg and vanilla. Beat until smooth.

4. Roll out half of the dough to a 15 x 12-inch rectangle. Spread with half of the creamed filling. Sprinkle with 1/2 cup nuts. Cut into three 12 x 5-inch strips. Roll each as for a jelly roll, starting with the 12-inch side. Pinch to seal. Braid the 3 rolls. Place in a greased loaf pan. Repeat with remaining dough, filling and nuts. Cover and let rise until double (1/2-1 hour).

5. Preheat oven to 325°.

6. Brush tops with slightly beaten egg white diluted with water. Sprinkle with granulated sugar. Bake 40-50 minutes until golden brown.

Makes 2 loaves   S Joanne Vallero, CSJ

Note: This bread is a traditional favorite in the Vallero family. It is often baked for holidays and for gift giving.

Spring Breads

GREEN MEADOWS' BRAN MUFFINS

6 cups All-Bran cereal, divided into 2 and 4 cups	4 cups buttermilk
2 cups boiling water	5 cups flour
2 cups sugar	1 teaspoon salt
1 cup margarine	5 teaspoons baking soda
4 eggs	3 cups raisins
	3 cups nuts

1. Preheat oven to 400°.
2. Mix 2 cups All-Bran and boiling water. Set aside to cool.
3. In large bowl, beat sugar and margarine. Add eggs and buttermilk. Beat in cooled bran. Mix well. Set aside.
4. Combine flour, salt, baking soda and remaining 4 cups of All-Bran. Add to liquid ingredients. Add raisins and nuts.
5. Spoon into greased muffin pans until two-thirds full. Bake for 20 minutes. Serve hot.

Makes 4 1/2 dozen muffins   *Marjorie Johnson*

Note: If only a few muffins are to be made, the remaining batter will keep in the refrigerator for 2 weeks.

RHUBARB BREAD

1 1/2 cups brown sugar	2 1/2 cups flour
2/3 cup vegetable oil	1 1/2 cups rhubarb, finely chopped
1 egg	*Topping:*
1 cup buttermilk	1 tablespoon butter
1 teaspoon baking soda	1/2 cup sugar
1 teaspoon salt	1 teaspoon ground cinnamon
1 teaspoon vanilla	

1. Preheat oven to 350°.
2. Mix together brown sugar, oil, egg, buttermilk, baking soda, salt and vanilla. Add flour. Stir in rhubarb. Pour into 2 greased loaf pans.
3. Combine butter, sugar and cinnamon for topping. Spread on loaves.
4. Bake 40 minutes, until toothpick inserted in center comes out clean. Remove from pans. Cool on racks.

Makes 2 loaves   *Vel Ball*

Spring Breads

SWEET IRISH CREAM BREAD

2 (3 oz.) packages light cream cheese, softened	1/3 cup Irish Cream liqueur
1/4 cup sugar	1 tablespoon vegetable oil
2 eggs, divided	*Glaze:*
1 package quick date bread mix	1/2 cup powdered sugar
2/3 cup water	1 tablespoon Irish Cream liqueur
	2 teaspoons milk

1. Preheat oven to 350°. Grease and flour bottom of loaf pan.

2. Prepare filling by blending cream cheese, sugar and 1 egg. Blend with mixer until smooth. Set aside.

3. In large bowl prepare bread mix by combining package contents with water, Irish Cream, oil and remaining egg. Stir by hand until moistened.

4. Pour 1 cup batter into loaf pan. Spoon cream cheese filling over batter. Pour in remaining batter. Marbleize the bread by pulling a knife through batter in figure-eight patterns. Bake 65-75 minutes. Remove from pan. Cool.

5. Mix glaze ingredients and drizzle over loaf.

Serves 12   *LaVerne Maher*

GRANDMA GOLDIE'S COFFEE CAKE

Crust:
1 cup flour
1/2 cup butter
2 tablespoons water

Filling:
1 cup water
1/2 cup butter
1 cup flour
3 eggs
1/2 teaspoon almond extract

Frosting:
1/2 cup butter, softened
1 pound powdered sugar
1 teaspoon vanilla
4 tablespoons heavy cream as needed
pecans, chopped

1. Preheat oven to 350°.

2. For crust: Cut butter into flour with pastry blender. Stir in water. Pat dough onto 11 x 15-inch jelly roll pan.

3. For filling: Bring water and butter to boil. Remove from heat. Stir in flour all at once to form a ball. Cool. Beat in eggs, one at a time. Stir in almond extract. Spread on top of crust. Bake 45-50 minutes. Cool.

4. For frosting: Beat butter and vanilla into powdered sugar. Whip in as much cream as needed to spread. Spread on cooled cake. Sprinkle with nuts.

Makes 36 bars   *Goldie Anderson*

Spring Breads

CREAM CHEESE COFFEE CAKE

Regular Crust:
- 1 cup margarine
- 2 1/2 cups flour
- 1 tablespoon sugar
- 1 package dry yeast
- 5 tablespoons milk
- 4 egg yolks, beaten
- 2 egg whites
- 1/2 cup nuts, chopped

Filling:
- 2 (8 oz.) packages cream cheese
- 1 cup sugar
- 1 egg yolk
- 1 teaspoon vanilla

Glaze:
- 1 cup powdered sugar
- 2 tablespoons milk
- 1/2 teaspoon vanilla

REGULAR CRUST:
1. Combine margarine, flour, sugar and yeast.
2. Scald milk. Cool to 110°. Combine milk and egg yolks with flour mixture.
3. Prepare filling: Beat cream cheese and sugar. Add egg yolk and vanilla.
4. Divide dough in half. Roll each half between waxed paper dusted with flour to a 9 x 13-inch rectangle. Press dough into greased 9 x 13-inch pan. Spread filling on top. Place second sheet of rolled dough on top of filling. Cover with plastic wrap and let rise 3 hours in a warm place. (It never really rises.)
5. Preheat oven to 350°. Beat 2 egg whites until foamy and spread on top of dough. Sprinkle with 1/2 cup nuts. Bake 30-40 minutes. Cool.
6. Mix glaze ingredients and drizzle over loaf. Refrigerate.

QUICK CRUST VARIATION

- 2 (8 oz.) tubes refrigerator crescent rolls
- 1 egg white
- 1/2 cup nuts, chopped

1. Preheat oven to 375°.
2. Press 1 tube of crescent rolls into greased 9 x 13-inch pan. Spread filling mixture over top of crescent rolls.
3. Turn out second crescent roll tube on lightly floured board. With rolling pin press dough to a 9 x 13-inch shape. Place on top of filling. Stretch to form edges.
4. Beat egg white and brush on top of dough. Sprinkle with nuts. Bake 25 minutes. Cool. Mix glaze ingredients and drizzle over loaf. Refrigerate until serving time.

Makes 16-24 pieces

Sally DeCardy
Shirley Yuill

*Spring
Appetizers*

GOAT CHEESE SPREAD WITH TOMATOES

4 cloves garlic, unpeeled
4 ounces goat cheese
1 cup fresh plum tomatoes, peeled, seeded and diced
1/2 cup red onion, diced
1/4 cup olive oil
6 tablespoons balsamic vinegar
3 tablespoons fresh basil, chopped

1. Preheat oven to 350°.

2. Wrap garlic in foil and bake 15 minutes until soft.

3. Squeeze garlic from skin and mash with fork. Beat garlic and goat cheese until smooth. Shape cheese mixture into mound in a microwave-safe dish.

4. In a bowl toss together tomatoes, onion, basil, oil and vinegar.

5. To serve: Warm cheese in microwave oven. Place warmed cheese in the center of a serving platter and spoon the tomato mixture over the goat cheese. Serve toast points or crackers on the side. Provide a wide knife to spread mixture.

Serves 4

Ron and Jackie Gall

MARINATED SHRIMP

2 pounds cooked shrimp, peeled and deveined, with tail intact
2 medium Vidalia onions, thinly sliced
4 bay leaves
2 lemons, thinly sliced
2-3 tablespoons fresh oregano, chopped
1 cup extra virgin olive oil
1/4 cup fresh lemon juice
1/4 cup white wine vinegar
2-3 tablespoons garlic, minced
2 teaspoons black peppercorns
1 teaspoon mustard seed
1 tablespoon salt

1. Combine all ingredients except shrimp to make a marinade.

2. Pour marinade over shrimp, making sure the shrimp are completely submerged. Cover and refrigerate for 48 hours, stirring occasionally.

3. Serve shrimp and onions, drizzled with marinade.

Serves 4-6 as appetizer

Jan F. Kohl

17

Spring Appetizers

SPINACH AND CHEESE APPETIZERS

    3 (10 oz.) packages frozen chopped spinach, thawed and squeezed dry
    1 pound feta cheese, crumbled
    4 ounces mozzarella cheese, or brick cheese, shredded
    3 bunches green onions, chopped
    1 tablespoon olive oil
    1 tablespoon water
    1 pound filo dough, at room temperature for 1 hour
    2 tablespoons dried dill
       freshly ground pepper to taste
       vegetable oil

1. Saute green onions in olive oil and water until tender. Do not brown.

2. In bowl combine spinach, sauteed green onions, dill and pepper. Add crumbled feta cheese and mozzarella cheese. Stir well. Divide filling into 7 portions.

3. Preheat oven to 350°.

4. Brush 1 sheet of filo lightly with oil. Lay second sheet on top. Brush again with oil. Spread 1/7 of the filling across the narrow end. Roll up like a jelly roll. Use a third sheet of oiled filo rolled around the already filled roll, tucking the ends under. Repeat for remaining 6 portions of filling.

5. Place rolls in an oiled pan and bake 45 minutes or until golden.

6. To serve, cut diagonally into 1 1/2-inch pieces and arrange on serving dish.

Makes 63 appetizers   *Patty Dritsas*

Note: Assembled appetizer may be frozen. Bake an additional 15 minutes if frozen. May also be used as a side dish by cutting slightly thicker.

Spring Appetizers

TANGY APRICOT APPETIZER

1 cup white wine	1/2 teaspoon dry mustard
1/2 cup dry apricots	1/2 cup red pepper, chopped
1 cup apricot preserves	1 (8 oz.) package cream cheese,
2 tablespoons horseradish	Brie or Camembert
hot sauce to taste	

1. Cook apricots in wine until wine is absorbed.
2. Pulse in food processor, retaining chunky texture.
3. Add apricot preserves, hot sauce, horseradish and mustard. Pulse to blend.
4. Add red pepper to processor. Pulse 2-3 times to blend.
5. Best made ahead and refrigerated. Serve over cream cheese, warm Brie or Camembert.

Makes 2 cups   *Roberta Sprowl, Penny Newkirk*

Note: Recipe may be thinned with 1/2 cup of white wine to use as a glaze for grilled chicken breasts.

SHRIMP CHEESE APPETIZERS

6 English muffins	1/2 teaspoon seasoned salt
1 (5 oz.) jar Old English Cheese Spread	1/2 teaspoon garlic powder
1/4 cup margarine	1/4 teaspoon lemon pepper
1 tablespoon mayonnaise	1 (12 oz.) bag frozen shrimp, thawed

1. Drain shrimp on paper towel to remove excess moisture.
2. Mix cheese, margarine, mayonnaise and seasonings. Stir in half of the shrimp. Spread on muffin halves and freeze on a baking sheet.
3. Preheat oven to 400°.
4. Cut each muffin half into 6 wedges. Bake 5-8 minutes. Garnish tops with remaining shrimp and place under broiler. Broil until bubbly and golden brown.

Makes 72 pieces   *Joyce Currie*

Spring Soups

EASTER HAM AND BEAN SOUP

- 1 leftover honey-glazed ham bone, with some meat attached
- 1 pound mixed dried beans
- 2 quarts water
- 1 quart chicken broth
- 1 teaspoon chili powder
- 1 1/2 cups celery, chopped
- 1 1/2 cups onion, chopped
- 1 (28 oz.) can chopped tomatoes
- 2 tablespoons dried parsley
- pepper

1. Remove as much fat as possible from ham bone. Rinse and sort beans. Throw away flavor packet, if included with beans.

2. In large soup pot combine beans and water. Cover and boil 1 hour. Let stand 1 hour.

3. Add remaining ingredients. Simmer 1-2 hours until beans are tender, stirring often.

4. Remove ham bone. Cool. Remove meat from bone and add to soup. Simmer 30 minutes, adding water as necessary for desired thickness.

Serves 8   *Carleen Bart*

ASPARAGUS SOUP

- 2 pounds fresh asparagus
- 6 tablespoons butter
- 1 bunch green onions, chopped
- 8 tablespoons flour (6 tablespoons if serving cold)
- 6 cups chicken broth, divided
- 1 cup half-and-half
- 1/2 cup fresh parsley, finely chopped
- white pepper to taste
- 1/4 teaspoon dried thyme

1. Cut off top 3 inches of asparagus tips. Save. Trim remaining stalks into 1/2-inch pieces and simmer covered with water approximately 40 minutes until very tender. Cook tips separately just until tender, approximately 3 minutes.

2. Melt butter in stockpot. Add onions and saute until translucent. Add flour and stir until smooth. Cook and stir 2-3 minutes. This will be a firm paste. Add 4 cups chicken broth, a small amount at a time. Whisk until smooth. Simmer and stir until thickened.

3. Puree asparagus stalk bottoms in food processor with 2 remaining cups of chicken broth. Process until liquefied. Force through a fine sieve into stockpot.

4. Add small amount of hot soup to half-and-half. Return to stockpot.

5. Add seasonings, parsley and asparagus tips (cut into 1/2-inch pieces). Simmer. Do not let soup come to a boil.

Serves 4-6   *Penny Newkirk*

Spring Salads

FRESH ASPARAGUS SALAD

2 pounds fresh asparagus	salt and pepper to taste
1 cup olive oil	1 jar roasted red pepper,
1/4 cup fresh lemon juice	drained and cut into strips
2 teaspoons balsamic vinegar	1 (DR.WT. 4.5 oz.) jar
2 tablespoons Dijon mustard	whole button mushrooms, drained

1. Trim asparagus to tender point. Peel ends if stalks are large. Cut into 3-inch long pieces, on a bias.

2. Bring a large pot of salted water to a rolling boil. Add the asparagus. Cover. Cook for 2 minutes. Drain. Rinse with cold water until the asparagus is no longer hot. Allow to drain while preparing vinaigrette.

3. Mix together olive oil, lemon juice and balsamic vinegar. Whisk in mustard. Season to taste with salt and pepper.

4. Combine asparagus, red pepper strips and mushrooms in bowl. Add vinaigrette. Toss to coat evenly. Serve at room temperature.

Serves 8 *Fern Bart*

Note: Cherry tomato halves and freshly grated Parmesan cheese may also be added.

ORIENTAL SPINACH SALAD

1/4 package fresh spinach, cleaned, rinsed and dried	*Dressing:*
2 heads lettuce	2/3 cup sugar
2 (6 oz.) cans mandarin oranges	5 tablespoons lemon juice
1 red onion, thinly sliced	5 tablespoons honey
5-6 slices bacon, fried, drained and crumbled	1/2 cup red wine vinegar
1 (4 oz.) package slivered almonds	1 teaspoon paprika
	1 teaspoon celery seed
	1 teaspoon salt
	1 cup vegetable oil

1. Mix dressing ingredients. Refrigerate.

2. Prepare lettuce and spinach in salad bowl. Add oranges, onion and bacon. Refrigerate until served.

3. Just before serving toss dressing with salad. Garnish with slivered almonds.

Serves 12 *Ron and Jackie Gall*

Spring Salads

DULUTH POPPY SEED DRESSING

 3/4 cup sugar
 1 teaspoon dry mustard
 1 teaspoon salt
 1/3 cup white wine vinegar
 2 tablespoons onion, chopped
 1 cup vegetable oil
 1 teaspoon poppy seed
 1 teaspoon sesame seed

1. In a blender or food processor combine sugar and onion until smooth. Add dry mustard, salt and vinegar.

2. With machine running, very slowly pour in oil. Process until thick and creamy. Stop machine and stir in poppy seed and sesame seed. If mixture gets too thick add 1-2 tablespoons water. Chill before serving.

Makes about 2 cups   *Carleen Bart*

Note: Red wine vinegar and red onion may be substituted for white wine vinegar and white onion for a nice pink color which looks great on fruit with greens.

BLUE CHEESE DRESSING

 1 1/2 cups mayonnaise
 3/4 cup sour cream
 1/2 teaspoon dry mustard
 1/4 teaspoon hot red pepper sauce
 1/2 teaspoon salt
 1 clove garlic, pressed
 2 teaspoons Worcestershire sauce
 4 ounces blue cheese, crumbled

1. Combine all ingredients except blue cheese in mixing bowl. Blend until smooth.

2. Mix in blue cheese and refrigerate overnight to blend flavors.

Makes 2 cups   *Penny Newkirk*

Spring Salads

MIXED GREENS WITH CREAMY RASPBERRY DRESSING

  4 cups mixed greens, torn
    (romaine, red and green leaf, Boston, Bibb, radicchio)
  1 can artichoke hearts, halved
  1/2 cup walnuts, coarsely chopped

Dressing:
  1/3 cup vegetable oil
  3 tablespoons sugar
  2 tablespoons raspberry or red wine vinegar
  1 tablespoon sour cream
 1 1/2 teaspoons Dijon mustard
  1/2 cup fresh raspberries, reserving a few for garnish

1. Combine first 5 dressing ingredients. Gently fold in raspberries.

2. Arrange greens on individual plates. Top with artichoke halves. Drizzle with dressing and sprinkle with nuts and a few extra raspberries.

Serves 4   *Carleen Bart*

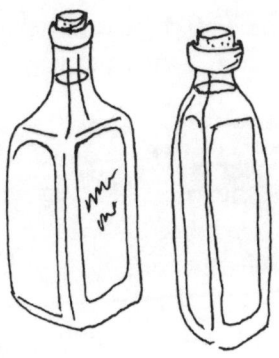

*Spring
Side Dishes*

ASPARAGUS TIMBALES

 1/4 cup dry bread crumbs, crushed
 1/2 cup onion, finely minced
 1 tablespoon butter
 1/2 cup Swiss cheese, grated
 5 eggs
 1 cup milk
 4 tablespoons butter
 2/3 cup bread crumbs
 1/4 teaspoon salt
    dash fresh nutmeg
    pinch of salt
    pinch of white pepper
 3 cups asparagus, cooked,
    cut into 1/2-inch pieces

1. Preheat oven to 325°.

2. Oil timbale molds and cover the surface with bread crumbs. Tap out excess crumbs.

3. Cook the onion in butter just until translucent. Put in mixing bowl and add seasonings, cheese and 2/3 cup bread crumbs.

4. Heat milk with 4 tablespoons butter to just below boiling. Beat eggs and add warmed milk, a small amount at a time. Add asparagus.

5. Put egg and asparagus mixture into prepared molds, set into boiling water bath and place in lower third of oven. Bake 25-30 minutes or until knife inserted in center comes out clean. When ready to serve, run knife around edge and invert mold onto serving dish. May be kept warm in boiling water bath. Serve with hollandaise if desired.

Serves 6-8 (2-3 oz. timbale molds)   *Penny Newkirk*

*Spring
Side Dishes*

ASPARAGUS CASSEROLE

12 ounces fresh mushrooms, cleaned and sliced	1/2 teaspoon salt
1 cup onion, chopped	1/4 teaspoon fresh nutmeg
1/4 cup plus 1 tablespoon margarine	1 cup milk
2 tablespoons flour	1 pound fresh asparagus, cut into 2-inch pieces
1 teaspoon chicken base or bouillon granules	1/4 cup bread crumbs

1. Preheat oven to 350°.
2. Saute mushrooms and onion in 1/4 cup margarine until onion is translucent.
3. Blend in flour. Add milk, chicken base, salt and nutmeg. Cook until thickened.
4. Cook asparagus 5-7 minutes in boiling water. Drain.
5. Combine asparagus with mushroom-onion mixture in 1 1/2-quart greased casserole.
6. Combine bread crumbs with 1 tablespoon of melted margarine. Sprinkle on top of casserole. Bake uncovered 30-40 minutes.

Serves 4-6   *Penny Newkirk*

VIDALIA ONION CLASSIC CASSEROLE

4 large Vidalia onions, sliced	2 tablespoons flour
1/2 cup butter or margarine	1/2 cup soft bread crumbs
2/3 cup chicken broth	1/2 cup Cheddar cheese, grated
1/3 cup sherry	2 tablespoons Parmesan cheese

1. Preheat oven to 350°.
2. Saute onions in butter or margarine until soft and translucent.
3. Add flour, broth and sherry to skillet. Stir and cook until thickened.
4. Put in buttered casserole. Top with bread crumbs and cheeses. Bake 20 minutes or until lightly browned and bubbly.

Serves 6-8   *Roberta Sprowl*

Note: This is a great accompaniment for roasted or grilled meats.

*Spring
Side Dishes*

CHEDDAR POTATO AUGRATIN

   8 *large potatoes, cooked and peeled*   1 *teaspoon garlic, minced*
   4 *tablespoons flour*   1/2 *teaspoon paprika*
   4 *tablespoons butter*   1/4 *teaspoon salt*
   2 *cups milk*   *freshly ground pepper to taste*
   2 *cups Cheddar cheese, shredded*

1. Cut potatoes into large chunks and place in a buttered casserole. Set aside.

2. Melt butter in a saucepan. Whisk in flour. Blend well. Gradually add the milk while whisking. When the mixture comes to a boil lower the heat and add cheese, garlic, paprika, salt and pepper.

3. Preheat oven to 350°.

4. Pour mixture over potatoes. Sprinkle paprika over top. Bake 40-45 minutes until lightly browned and bubbling.

Serves 8-10   *Carol Bushnell*

GRECIAN BROCCOLI RICE

   1 *cup raw rice*
   2 *tablespoons olive oil*
   4 *garlic cloves, minced*
   2 *medium tomatoes, cored, seeded and diced*
   1 *bunch broccoli, cut into florets (5 cups)*
  1/2 *teaspoon dried oregano*
  1/4 *cup water*
   5 *ounces feta cheese, crumbled*
      freshly ground pepper to taste

1. Cook rice according to package directions.

2. Heat olive oil in large skillet. Saute garlic 2 minutes. Add tomatoes and saute 2 minutes. Add broccoli and oregano and toss.

3. Pour in water and cover. Cook 5 minutes.

4. Stir in hot rice, feta cheese and pepper to taste.

Serves 6-8   *Vel Ball*

Spring Entrees

CHINESE PEPPER STEAK

   1   pound beef sirloin, sliced 1/4-inch thick
   2   tablespoons vegetable oil
  1/2 teaspoon dried marjoram or oregano
  1/2 teaspoon dried basil
  1/4 teaspoon freshly ground pepper
   3   tablespoons soy sauce
  1/4 cup whiskey
 1-2 cloves garlic, pressed
   3   red peppers, cut in strips
   3   green peppers, cut in strips
   6   medium-size firm tomatoes, quartered
   1   onion, sliced
  1/2 pound whole fresh mushrooms
       cornstarch and water for thickening as needed

1. In a wok brown meat in oil 3 minutes on each side. Add seasonings, soy sauce, whiskey and garlic. Cover and cook at medium heat 5-6 minutes, turning once.

2. Add vegetables and cook about 7 minutes more, turning and mixing constantly, until vegetables are heated through and are still crisp and colorful. If necessary thicken with a little cornstarch dissolved in 1/4 cup cold water. Serve over rice.

Serves 4-6   *Mickey Lubcke*

Note: 1 (28 oz.) can plum tomatoes, drained and quartered, may be used instead of fresh.

Spring Entrees

IRISH CORNED BEEF

5 pounds corned beef
2 (12 oz.) cans beer
2 whole cloves garlic, peeled
1 bay leaf
1 teaspoon whole peppercorns
2 whole onions, peeled
1 teaspoon paprika
1/2 cup Irish whiskey
1/2 cup brown sugar

1. Wash beef well in cold water. Place in heavy pot, preferably one with a rack in bottom.

2. Pour in beer, then enough water just to cover meat. Add garlic, bay leaf, peppercorns and onions. Cover and bring to a boil, then turn down and simmer 45-60 minutes per pound or until tender.

3. Meat must be submerged in water while cooking, so add more water and beer (half and half) as needed. Be sure to keep temperature below boiling point while cooking or meat will be tough.

4. Keep cover on and let meat stand in liquid for 1 hour after cooking.

5. Preheat oven to 400°.

6. Place meat in a roasting pan. Sprinkle with paprika, whiskey and brown sugar, in that order. Bake for 20 minutes, basting every 5 minutes with 1/4 to 1/2 cup of liquid in which corned beef was boiled.

Serves 8   *Mickey Lubcke*

Note: Good served with boiled cabbage and new potatoes.

Spring Entrees

CHILI QUICHE

1/2 cup butter, melted	2 (4 oz.) cans chopped green chilies
10 eggs	2 cups cottage cheese
1/2 cup flour	1 pound Monterey Jack cheese, grated
1 teaspoon baking powder	1 teaspoon salt

1. Preheat oven to 400°.

2. Grease a 10 x 15 x 2-inch pan.

3. Beat eggs and add flour, baking powder and salt. Add butter, chilies, cottage cheese and Monterey Jack cheese. Mix well. Pour into prepared pan.

4. Bake for 15 minutes. Reduce heat to 350° and bake an additional 30-40 minutes, or until knife inserted in center comes out clean. Cut into squares and serve hot.

Serves 8
12-20 for appetizers

Joan C. Boeman
Mary Lou Conley

CHICKEN VELDENE

6 cups French bread, cubed into 1-inch pieces	2 cups milk
2 cups chicken or ham, cooked and shredded	1/4 cup Dijon mustard
2 cups fresh mushrooms, sliced	1/3 cup chicken broth
1 1/2 cups Cheddar cheese, shredded	1/2 cup green onion, chopped
1 1/2 cups mozzarella cheese, shredded	1/4 teaspoon pepper
10 eggs	

1. Place bread in greased 9 x 13-inch pan. Layer chicken, mushrooms and cheeses.

2. Whisk together eggs, milk, mustard and chicken broth. Add green onion and pepper. Pour over layered chicken mixture. Cover and refrigerate 6 hours or overnight.

3. Preheat oven to 325°.

4. Uncover and bake for 50-60 minutes or until set in center.

Serves 6-8

Vel Ball

Spring Entrees

COUNTRY CAPTAIN

- 4 chicken breast halves, cut into 1-inch cubes
- 2 tablespoons vegetable oil
- 1/3 cup onion, finely chopped
- 1/3 cup green bell pepper, finely chopped
- 1 clove garlic, crushed
- curry powder to taste
- 1/2 teaspoon dried thyme
- 2 tablespoons flour
- 1 teaspoon salt
- 1/4 teaspoon freshly ground pepper
- 2 cups canned stewed tomatoes, including liquid
- 3 tablespoons dried currants, optional
- 1 cup chicken broth as needed

1. Heat oil in a large skillet. Brown chicken on all sides. Remove chicken.
2. Add onion, green pepper, garlic, curry powder and thyme. Saute until onion wilts. Sprinkle vegetables with flour and cook for about 3 minutes.
3. Add tomatoes and cook until thickened. Add chicken broth if dry. Season with salt and pepper.
4. Return chicken to pan. Cover and cook until tender, about 20 minutes.
5. Stir currants into sauce and cook briefly until plump. Serve hot with rice.

Serves 4   *Ron and Jackie Gall*

MANDARIN CHICKEN BREASTS

- 4 chicken breast halves, skinned and boned
- vegetable cooking spray
- 2 teaspoons vegetable oil
- 1 (11 oz.) can mandarin oranges, undrained
- 3 tablespoons firmly packed brown sugar
- 1 teaspoon prepared mustard
- 2 small green onions, chopped
- 3 tablespoons catsup
- 1 tablespoon vinegar
- 1 teaspoon cornstarch
- 1/2 teaspoon ground cinnamon
- 1/8 teaspoon ground cloves

1. Coat large skillet with cooking spray and preheat over medium high heat. Add oil.
2. Lightly brown chicken, 2-3 minutes on each side.
3. Drain oranges, reserving juice. Set oranges aside. Combine juice and remaining ingredients, stir well and pour over chicken.
4. Cover and simmer 30 minutes. Add reserved mandarin oranges and simmer an additional 5 minutes or until chicken is tender.

Serves 4   *Marilyn Hendry*

Spring Entrees

SPINACH TERRINE

3 (10 oz.) packages frozen chopped spinach, thawed and squeezed dry
1 pound pork sausage, ground
salt to taste
1 cup onion, chopped
1 cup dry bread crumbs
6 eggs, beaten
1/4 teaspoon ground nutmeg
6 tablespoons heavy cream
1 cup Parmesan cheese, grated

1. Preheat oven to 350°.

2. Fry sausage slowly until lightly browned. Drain on paper towels. Saute onion in sausage fat until tender. Remove from pan.

3. Combine spinach, sausage and onion in bowl. Add bread crumbs, eggs, cream, nutmeg, cheese and salt. Blend all ingredients.

4. Grease the bottom and sides of a 5 x 9-inch loaf pan. Place mixture in pan and shape into loaf. Place loaf pan in shallow pan of hot water and bake 1 hour and 15 minutes or until internal temperature reaches 160°. Let stand 5 minutes before unmolding.

Makes 12 slices   *Marilyn Hendry*

Note: This is a wonderful brunch or side dish.

JOHN'S RACK OF LAMB

2 racks of lamb, French
1/2 cup fresh Italian parsley, chopped
1 cup Dijon mustard
1 cup plain bread crumbs

1. When preparing rack of lamb it is critical to remove all the fat from the rack. This means throwing away almost half of what is a costly cut of meat. Some butchers can French the rack for you. You will be left with a perfect loin of lamb with 8 or 9 ribs attached and end bones exposed.

2. Preheat oven to 400°. Position oven shelf in the middle of the oven.

3. Smear the racks liberally with mustard, then roll in a mixture of bread crumbs and Italian parsley.

4. Place the racks on a rimmed cookie sheet and bake for 18 minutes or until the center of lamb is pink. Remove from oven and let lamb set up for 5 minutes. Slice lamb between bones and serve each person 4-5 ribs.

Serves 4   *John and Jan F. Kohl*

Spring Entrees

HAWAIIAN CHICKEN

   1/2 cup butter or margarine, divided
    8 chicken breast halves, skinned and boned
        salt and pepper
    1 cup orange juice
    2 tablespoons lemon juice
  1/2 cup brown sugar
    1 tablespoon soy sauce
    2 tablespoons cornstarch
    1 fresh pineapple, peeled, cored and sliced
        or 1 (16 oz.) can pineapple chunks, drained
    1 green pepper, seeded and sliced
 1-2 fresh papayas, peeled, seeded and sliced
    1 mango, peeled and cubed
    1 medium onion, cut into chunks

1. Preheat oven to 350°.

2. Brown chicken in 1/4 cup melted butter. Place in a 9 x 13-inch baking dish. Season with salt and pepper. Brush chicken with remaining butter. Bake for 40 minutes.

3. Combine juices, brown sugar, soy sauce and cornstarch in a saucepan. Cook, stirring constantly, until thickened. Stir in fruits, onion and green pepper. Pour over chicken.

4. Bake 15 minutes longer or until chicken is tender. Serve with rice.

Serves 6   *Mi Loran*

Spring Entrees

LAMB KEBABS AND BALSAMIC VINEGAR

1 leg of lamb, cut into 1-inch cubes, 6-8 ounces per serving
peppers, cut into 2-inch pieces
onions, quartered
cherry tomatoes

Marinade:
2/3 cup olive oil
3 tablespoons fresh lemon juice
3 green onions, minced
3 large cloves garlic, minced
1 tablespoon fresh mint, chopped
1 tablespoon fresh rosemary, chopped
1 tablespoon fresh parsley, chopped
salt and pepper to taste

Vinaigrette:
2 fresh tomatoes, seeded and chopped
1/2 cup onion, finely diced
1 tablespoon fresh parsley, minced
1/3 cup olive oil
1/4 cup balsamic vinegar
2 cloves garlic, minced
1 teaspoon sugar
salt and pepper to taste

1. Prepare marinade for lamb by combining 2/3 cup olive oil, lemon juice, green onions, garlic, mint, rosemary, parsley, salt and pepper. Mix well and pour over meat. Allow to marinate in refrigerator overnight.

2. Prepare vinaigrette by combining tomatoes, onion, parsley, garlic, 1/3 cup olive oil, vinegar and sugar. Season with salt and pepper, and mix well. Set aside.

3. Place the marinated lamb on skewers alternating with peppers, onions and cherry tomatoes.

4. Grill in broiler or over hot coals for approximately 12-14 minutes. Spoon vinaigrette over kebabs when serving. Accompany with rice pilaf.

Serves 8   *Ron and Jackie Gall*

Spring Desserts

RHUBARB CUSTARD SQUARES

Crust:
- 4 cups all-purpose flour
- 1 1/2 teaspoons salt
- 2/3 cup butter flavor solid vegetable shortening
- 3/4 cup white vegetable shortening
- 1/2 cup plus 1 tablespoon water

Filling:
- 5 eggs
- 6 tablespoons milk
- 3 1/4 cups sugar
- 1/2 cup flour
- 1 teaspoon ground nutmeg
- 7 cups rhubarb, cut into 1/2-inch pieces
- 2 tablespoons margarine
- cinnamon sugar mixture to taste

1. Preheat oven to 400°.

2. For crust: Combine flour and salt. Cut in both shortenings. Sprinkle in water while blending with a fork. Chill in refrigerator.

3. For filling: Combine eggs and milk. Add sugar, flour and nutmeg. Add rhubarb.

4. To assemble: Roll two-thirds of dough to fit 10 x 15-inch jelly roll pan. Arrange in pan, pressing into corners and up sides. Pour in filling. Dot with margarine. Roll remaining crust, cut into strips and arrange a lattice top over filling. Tuck edges under bottom crust and crimp edges. Sprinkle top with cinnamon sugar to taste.

5. Bake 70 minutes until crust is golden brown and filling bubbles in middle. Put a strip of foil around edge of crust for the first 50 minutes of baking time to prevent over-browning.

Makes 20-24 squares   *Marge Mennerick*

*Spring
Desserts*

RHUBARB APPLE SQUARES

Crust:
- 2 1/2 cups flour
- 1 teaspoon salt
- 1 tablespoon sugar
- 1 cup shortening
- 1 egg yolk
- 1/2 cup milk as needed

Filling:
- 1 cup cornflakes, crushed
- 2 cups apples, peeled and sliced
- 2 cups rhubarb, cut into 1/4-inch pieces
  (or use 4 cups rhubarb and no apples)

Sauce:
- 2 cups sugar
- 2 cups water
- 4 tablespoons cornstarch
- 1 teaspoon vanilla
- 1/2 cup brown sugar
- 1 teaspoon ground cinnamon

Topping:
- 1 egg white
- 1 tablespoon sugar
- 1 tablespoon water

1. Preheat oven to 350°.

2. Prepare sauce: Stir cornstarch into 2 cups sugar. Add water. Boil until thickened, stirring as it heats. Stir in vanilla, brown sugar and cinnamon. Cool.

3. Prepare crust: Cut shortening into flour, salt and sugar using pastry blender or 2 knives. Beat egg yolk and add enough milk to make 2/3 cup. Add to flour mixture, stirring just until moistened. On floured work surface roll half of dough to fit bottom and sides of 11 x 15-inch jelly roll pan. Trim and piece if necessary. Cover with crushed cornflakes.

4. Arrange apple slices and rhubarb evenly over crust. Pour thickened sauce over top.

5. Roll remaining dough to fit and place over fruit and sauce. Tuck top crust between pan and bottom crust along edges. Seal with a fork. Beat egg white and water until frothy. Spread on top of crust. Sprinkle with sugar.

6. Bake 60 minutes. Cut into squares and serve while warm. Add a scoop of vanilla ice cream on top if desired.

Makes 20-24 bars   *Susan Kreager*

Spring Desserts

RHUBARB CRUNCH CAKE

2 cups flour	1/3 cup milk
1 1/4 cups sugar	2 cups rhubarb, cut into 1/2-inch pieces
1 teaspoon baking soda	
1 teaspoon salt	*Topping:*
1 teaspoon ground cinnamon	2/3 cup flour
1/4 teaspoon ground allspice	1/4 cup butter
1/4 teaspoon ground cloves	3/4 cup flaked coconut
2 eggs	1/4 cup nuts, chopped
1/2 cup vegetable oil	1/2 cup brown sugar

1. Preheat oven to 350°.
2. Combine flour, sugar, baking soda, salt, cinnamon, allspice and cloves.
3. In a separate bowl combine oil, eggs and milk. Stir liquids into dry ingredients. Stir in rhubarb. Spread batter into a greased and floured 9 x 13-inch baking pan.
4. Prepare topping: Cut butter into flour and brown sugar. Stir in coconut and nuts until mixture is crumbly. Sprinkle on top of cake batter.
5. Bake 40-45 minutes or until toothpick inserted into center comes out clean.

Makes 20-24 pieces *Barbara Taff*

CHOCOLATE DEADLIES

1/2 cup butter	*Frosting:*
1 cup sugar	5 tablespoons butter
1 1/2 squares unsweetened chocolate	1 square unsweetened chocolate
2/3 cup flour	2 cups powdered sugar
1 teaspoon vanilla	1/4 cup instant powdered coffee
2 eggs, beaten	
1 cup pecans, chopped	

1. Preheat oven to 350°.
2. Melt butter and chocolate. Add sugar, flour, eggs, vanilla and pecans. Mix well.
3. Fill miniature aluminum muffin cups with about a teaspoon of batter.
4. Bake for 15 minutes. Cool.
5. Prepare frosting: Melt butter with chocolate. Blend in powdered sugar and instant coffee until smooth. Frost.

Makes 3 dozen *Paula Brewer*

Spring
Desserts

ELEANOR'S OATMEALS

1/2 cup margarine	1 cup flour
1 teaspoon salt	3/4 teaspoon baking soda
1 teaspoon ground cinnamon	1 cup regular rolled oats
1 teaspoon vanilla	1/3 cup raisins
1 tablespoon molasses	1/3 cup dates, chopped
1 cup sugar	1/3 cup nuts, chopped
1 egg, beaten	

1. Preheat oven to 350°.
2. Combine shortening, salt, cinnamon, vanilla, molasses, sugar and egg. Beat thoroughly. Sift flour with baking soda. Add to first mixture. Mix well. Add oats, raisins, dates, and nuts. Mix well.
3. Drop by tablespoonfuls onto greased cookie sheet. Bake 10-15 minutes.

Makes 3 1/2 dozen cookies   *Eleanor Hoffman*

GREATEST SUGAR COOKIES

1 cup margarine or butter	4 cups flour
1 cup vegetable oil	1 teaspoon baking soda
1 cup sugar	1 teaspoon cream of tartar
1 cup powdered sugar	1 teaspoon salt
2 eggs	granulated sugar
1 teaspoon vanilla	

1. Preheat oven to 375°.
2. Cream oil, butter, sugar and powdered sugar. Add vanilla and eggs. Add flour, baking soda, cream of tartar and salt.
3. Shape dough into balls and roll in granulated sugar. Press down on greased cookie sheet with glass dipped in sugar.
4. Bake 12 minutes or until edges start to brown.

Makes 8 dozen cookies   *Eleanor Hoffman*
     Pat Kitner

Note: These are without a doubt the best sugar cookies, ever.

Spring Desserts

POLISH EASTER TORTE

1 1/4 cups unsalted butter
3/4 cup sugar
3 cups flour
6 egg yolks, hard-cooked
1/2 teaspoon lemon peel, grated
1 cup blanched almonds, finely ground
1/8 teaspoon ground nutmeg
12 ounces apricot preserves

Frosting:
1 1/2 cups powdered sugar
2 tablespoons butter, melted
1/8 teaspoon almond extract
1-2 tablespoons milk as needed
1/4 cup sliced almonds

1. Preheat oven to 325°. Grease four 9-inch round cake pans. Place flat circles of parchment paper in pans.

2. Cut butter into flour and sugar with pastry blender or 2 knives. Mash egg yolks and add to flour, sugar and butter mixture with lemon gratings, nutmeg and almonds. Stir to blend well and then by hand squeeze until dough almost sticks together.

3. Divide into the 4 prepared pans and press down evenly until a firm crust is formed.

4. Bake 15-18 minutes or until edges are just barely beginning to brown. Watch carefully. While it is still warm, turn first layer from pan onto cake plate. Remove parchment paper and spread with one-third of preserves. Layers are very crumbly and hard to handle. Turn second and third layers carefully over first layer, spreading preserves between layers. Add fourth layer. Cover and let stand at room temperature for 2 days before serving.

5. Prepare frosting: Beat powdered sugar, butter and almond extract, adding enough milk until mixture is smooth and creamy. Frost top of torte. Decorate with sliced almonds. To serve: Cut into 1-inch diamonds.

Serves 12-16   *Anne Kedzior Nordstrom*

Note: This is a Kedzior family tradition for 3 generations.

Spring
Desserts

HUMMINGBIRD CAKE

   3   cups flour
1/2 teaspoon salt
   1   teaspoon ground cinnamon
   1   teaspoon baking soda
   2   cups sugar
   3   eggs, beaten
3/4 cup vegetable oil
1 1/2 teaspoons vanilla
   1   (8 oz.) can crushed pineapple, undrained
1 3/4 cups ripe bananas, mashed
   1   cup flaked coconut
   1   cup pecans or walnuts, chopped

Cream Cheese Frosting:
1/2 cup butter or margarine, softened
   1   pound powdered sugar, sifted
1/2 cup pecans or walnuts, chopped
   1   (8 oz.) package cream cheese, softened
   1   teaspoon vanilla

1. Preheat oven to 350°. Grease and flour three 9-inch round cake pans.

2. Combine flour, salt, cinnamon, baking soda and sugar. Add eggs, oil and vanilla, stirring only until ingredients are moistened. Do not beat. Stir in pineapple, bananas, coconut and nuts.

3. Divide into 3 prepared pans. Bake for 23-28 minutes or until a toothpick inserted in center comes out clean.

4. Cool in pans 10 minutes. Remove cake layers from pans and cool completely on wire racks.

5. Prepare frosting: Cream butter and cream cheese. Gradually add powdered sugar and beat until light and fluffy. Stir in vanilla. Frost cake and sprinkle nuts on top.

Makes one 3-layer cake   *Carol Juntunen*

Spring Desserts

PINEAPPLE UPSIDE-DOWN CAKE

1/2 cup butter
1 1/4 cups brown sugar, packed
1 (8 oz.) can pineapple rings, drained
4 egg yolks
2/3 cup sugar
2/3 cup flour
4 egg whites, beaten until peaked
1 teaspoon baking powder
1/2 teaspoon salt
1 teaspoon lemon juice

1. Preheat oven to 350°.

2. Melt butter in bottom of 10-inch iron skillet or equally heavy oven-proof pan with straight sides. Sprinkle brown sugar across bottom. Arrange pineapple rings to cover brown sugar.

3. In mixing bowl, beat egg yolks until light and lemon colored. Add sugar and beat. Stir in 1/3 cup flour. Fold in half of the beaten egg whites. Stir baking powder and salt into remaining 1/3 cup of flour and fold into batter. Fold in remaining egg whites and lemon juice.

4. Pour batter on top of pineapple rings in iron skillet.

5. Bake 40-50 minutes until toothpick inserted into center comes out clean. Remove cake immediately by turning pan upside down onto serving platter.

Serves 8

Grandma Garrett
Jean McPartlin
Penny Newkirk

Note: Made and served by three generations of upside-down cake lovers.

Summer

Table of Contents

Appetizers
Breads
Soups
Salads
Side Dishes
Entrees
Desserts

Summer Appetizers

ANTIPASTO TORTORICE

- 1 (8 oz.) package cheese tortellini
- 1 basket cherry tomatoes
- 1 (15 oz.) can large pitted black olives
- 1 (15 oz.) can artichoke hearts, quartered
- 2 cups summer sausage, cut into 3/4-inch chunks
- 2 cups assorted cheeses, cut into 3/4-inch chunks
- 2-3 assorted peppers, cut into 1-inch chunks
- 1 cup pearl onions, canned or frozen
- 1 cup feta cheese, crumbled

Dressing:
- 1/4 cup olive oil
- 1/4 cup vegetable oil
- 1/2 cup red wine vinegar
- 1 teaspoon sugar
- 1 tablespoon Dijon mustard
- 1/2 teaspoon ground fennel seed
- 1 tablespoon lemon juice
- 1 tablespoon dried parsley
- 1/2 teaspoon salt
- freshly ground pepper
- 1/2 cup Parmesan cheese, grated

1. Cook tortellini according to package directions. Do not overcook. Drain and cool.
2. Blend all dressing ingredients.
3. Combine tortellini and remaining ingredients with dressing. Toss to coat. Refrigerate 2-4 hours before serving, stirring occasionally.
4. Drain off dressing. Serve on lettuce-lined platter or bowl, with toothpicks to spear pieces.

Serves 10 or more

Carleen Bart

Summer Appetizers

SALSA CILANTRO

 1 (14 oz.) can diced tomatoes
 1/2 cup onion, chopped
 1/2 cup green pepper, chopped
 1 large clove garlic, pressed
 1 tablespoon water
 2 tablespoons fresh lime juice
 1/2 cup fresh cilantro, chopped
  freshly ground pepper
 1 teaspoon salt
  hot sauce to taste

1. Combine onion, green pepper and garlic with 1 tablespoon of water. Microwave, covered with plastic wrap, on high power for 2 minutes.

2. Add cooked vegetables to the tomatoes, lime juice, cilantro, salt and pepper in bowl of food processor. Pulse to coarsely chop. Add hot sauce to taste.

3. Refrigerate several hours to blend flavors. Serve at room temperature.

Makes 2 cups   *Carleen Bart*

STRAWBERRY RUMBA

 12 ounces light frozen whipped topping,
    thawed and divided
 1/2 cup brown sugar, packed
 2 teaspoons vanilla
 1 teaspoon rum extract
   (or 1 tablespoon dark rum)
  fresh strawberries

Mix 1/2 cup whipped topping with brown sugar, vanilla and rum. Stir until well blended. Let stand 5 minutes until sugar dissolves. Stir again. Fold brown sugar mixture into remaining whipped topping. Serve with strawberries.

Makes 2 cups   *Carleen Bart*

Summer Appetizers

BOURSIN CHEESE

1/2 cup butter, cubed
1 (8 oz.) package cream cheese, cubed
1 clove garlic, peeled
1/4 teaspoon dried basil
1/4 teaspoon dried oregano
1/4 teaspoon dried thyme

1. Mince garlic in bowl of the food processor. Add butter and cream cheese. Process until smooth.

2. Add dried herbs to cream cheese mixture. Blend until smooth. Refrigerate until serving time.

Serving suggestions:

1. With vegetables or on crackers as an appetizer or snack

2. On a baked potato

3. In a chicken breast for chicken Kiev

4. On a vegetable sandwich or ham on rye

Makes 1 cup   *Cooking Craft*

Note: This spread will keep in refrigerator for as long as the freshness date shown on the cream cheese package.

SANGRIA

1 fifth dry red wine, chilled
2 ounces brandy
1/3 cup simple syrup
juice of 1 orange
1 lime, thinly sliced
1 lemon, thinly sliced
1 orange, thinly sliced
1 cup club soda, chilled
ice cubes
fruit slices for garnish

1. To make simple syrup for sangria combine equal amounts of water and sugar. Bring to a boil and cook until sugar is dissolved and mixture is clear. Cool.

2. In a large pitcher combine wine, brandy, 1/3 cup simple syrup and the juice of one orange. Add lime, lemon and orange slices.

3. Refrigerate no longer than 1 hour before serving. (Peels will make sangria bitter.)

4. To serve, add club soda to pitcher. Pour sangria over ice cubes in large wine glasses. Garnish with fruit slices.

Serves 6 *Virginia Hudson*

Summer Breads

BEAUMONDE BREAD

1 long loaf French bread or 2 twin loaves
1 tablespoon poppy seed
1 cup butter
1/2 teaspoon dry mustard
2 teaspoons Beaumonde seasoning, divided
1/4 cup green onion, minced
1 pound Lorraine Swiss cheese, sliced and halved

1. Preheat oven to 350°.
2. Cut bread along top diagonally but not all the way through. Poke cheese into slots of bread.
3. Melt butter. Add poppy seed, dry mustard, 1 1/2 teaspoons Beaumonde seasoning and onion.
4. Set bread on aluminum foil. Pour butter mixture over bread and sprinkle with remaining Beaumonde. Wrap bread in heavy foil and place on baking sheet. Bake for 30 minutes.

Serves 6-8   *Linda Howells*

Note: In place of Beaumonde seasoning 1 teaspoon minced garlic and 1 teaspoon celery seed may be used.

HERBED GARLIC BREAD

1 loaf French or Italian bread, sliced

Spread:
4 tablespoons butter, softened
1 clove garlic, minced
1 teaspoon dried parsley flakes
1/2 teaspoon ground oregano
1/2 teaspoon dried dill

1. Preheat oven to 425°.
2. Prepare spread: Blend together butter, garlic, parsley, oregano and dill. Spread on bread. Wrap loaf in foil. Bake 15-18 minutes or until warmed through.

Makes 1 loaf   *Penny Newkirk*

Note: This is also good spread on 1/4-inch thick sliced baguettes and baked on a cookie sheet until crisp to make brochettes for dips and spreads.

Summer Soups

FRESH TOMATO HERB SOUP

1/4 cup olive oil	2 tablespoons fresh parsley
2 medium onions, sliced	2 tablespoons fresh thyme
6 fresh medium tomatoes, peeled, cored and chopped	fresh dill to taste
	1 clove garlic, minced
1 (6 oz.) can tomato paste	4 cups chicken broth
3-4 tablespoons fresh basil	salt and pepper to taste

1. Saute onions in olive oil until tender and translucent.

2. Add tomatoes, tomato paste, broth, fresh herbs and spices. Bring to a boil. Reduce heat. Cover and simmer for 40 minutes.

3. Puree soup in a blender or food processor, a small amount at a time. Serve.

Serves 6-8   *Roberta Sprowl*

ZUCCHINI SOUP

1 pound hot Italian sausage	2 teaspoons salt
2 cups celery, cut into 1/2-inch pieces	1 tablespoon dried oregano
	1 tablespoon dried basil
1 quart beef broth	1 teaspoon sugar
2 pounds zucchini, cut into 1/2-inch pieces	5-6 cloves garlic, minced
	2 green peppers, cut into 1/2-inch pieces
1 cup onion, chopped	1/2 cup Parmesan cheese, grated
2 (28 oz.) cans chopped tomatoes with puree	mozzarella cheese, shredded

1. Brown sausage and celery. Drain.

2. Add beef broth, zucchini, onion, tomatoes, salt, oregano, basil, sugar and garlic. Cover and simmer 20 minutes. Add green peppers and Parmesan cheese. Simmer 10 minutes.

3. Pour soup into bowls and top with mozzarella cheese. Serve.

Serves 6-8   *Joyce Currie*

Summer Soups

JAN'S GAZPACHO

2	(48 oz.) cans low-sodium V-8 juice
1 1/2-2	ripe avocados, peeled and diced
3	cloves garlic, minced
10-12	green onions, chopped
1/2	red pepper, seeded and chopped into 1/4-inch cubes
1/2	yellow pepper, seeded and chopped into 1/4-inch cubes
1	cup celery, chopped
1	zucchini, chopped into 1/4-inch cubes
1	summer squash, chopped into 1/4-inch cubes
3	ears of corn, blanched for 1 minute, then kernels removed from cobs
4	vine ripened large tomatoes, seeded and chopped into 1/4-inch cubes
2-3	tablespoons fresh oregano (or 1 1/2 teaspoons dried)
1/2-3/4	cup fresh basil, chopped
1/2	teaspoon freshly ground pepper
2-3	tablespoons Worcestershire sauce to taste
2-3	shakes of hot sauce to taste
1/3	cup red wine vinegar
1/4	cup tarragon vinegar
2-3	tablespoons extra virgin olive oil
	salt to taste
	fresh chives

1. Combine all ingredients and refrigerate overnight.
2. Serve chilled, garnished with a sprinkling of fresh chives.

Makes 8 large servings   *Jan F. Kohl*

Note: This soup keeps in refrigerator up to 5 days.

Summer Salads

ARTICHOKE AND HEARTS OF PALM SALAD

- 2 (16 oz.) cans artichoke hearts, drained
- 2 (16 oz.) cans hearts of palm, drained
- 1 (2 oz.) jar chopped pimento or red pepper strips
- 3/4 cup olive oil
- 1 1/2 teaspoons ground cumin
- 1/2 cup sherry vinegar
- 3 cloves garlic, minced
- 5 teaspoons sugar or to taste
- 1 teaspoon salt
- freshly ground pepper to taste

1. Cut artichoke hearts in half. Cut hearts of palm into bite size pieces. Place artichoke hearts, hearts of palm and pimento or red pepper strips in serving bowl.

2. Combine together olive oil, cumin, vinegar, garlic, sugar, salt and pepper. Stir to blend. Pour dressing over artichokes and hearts of palm. Toss. Refrigerate several hours until serving time.

Serves 6-8

Penny Newkirk

BLACK BEAN AND FETA SALAD

- 2 (15 oz.) cans black beans, drained and rinsed
- 3/4 cup feta cheese, crumbled
- 1/3 cup red onion, minced
- 1/4 cup lemon juice
- 3 tablespoons olive oil
- 1/4 teaspoon salt
- 1/4 teaspoon freshly ground pepper

In a mixing bowl combine all the above ingredients. Toss gently. To blend flavors, cover and refrigerate for at least 30 minutes before serving.

Serves 10-12
relish size portions

Ron and Jackie Gall

Summer Salads

DANISH POTATO SALAD

8-10 medium potatoes	1 teaspoon Dijon mustard
1/2 cup mayonnaise	1 teaspoon curry powder
1/2 cup sour cream	salt and pepper to taste
1 cup green beans, cooked	

1. Boil potatoes in salted water until fork tender. Drain potatoes. Then cool, peel and cut them into chunks.

2. Blend mayonnaise, sour cream, mustard and curry powder together. Add salt and pepper to taste.

3. Add potatoes and green beans. Mix thoroughly. Refrigerate until served.

Serves 8   Diane Olsen

Note: "This recipe belongs to my mother-in-law who is from Sunderborg, Denmark. She often cooked for the Carlsburg Brewery family in Denmark."

PARIS POTATO SALAD

2 pounds medium new potatoes	1 tablespoon Dijon mustard
2 large green peppers, thinly sliced	1 clove garlic, pressed
1 small red onion, thinly sliced	1 1/2 teaspoons salt
1 (DR.WT. 4 oz.) can sliced mushrooms, drained	freshly ground pepper
1/2 red pepper, thinly sliced	1/4 cup black olives, sliced
3/4 cup olive or vegetable oil	2 tablespoons fresh parsley, chopped
3 tablespoons red wine vinegar	4 thick slices bacon, cooked and crumbled

1. Boil potatoes in salted water just until tender. Drain. Cut into 1/4-inch slices.

2. Combine potatoes, green peppers, onion, mushrooms, red pepper, olives and parsley.

3. Blend oil, vinegar, mustard, garlic, salt and pepper. Pour dressing over salad and toss lightly. Refrigerate 2-4 hours before serving. Garnish with bacon.

Serves 6-8   Carleen Bart

Summer Salads

FRUIT SALAD DRESSING

2 oranges, zested
2 lemons, zested
1 1/2 cups sugar
1/2 cup egg substitute

Juice oranges and lemons. Mix juices with sugar. Bring to a full boil. Remove from heat. Add egg substitute and fruit zests. Mix gently. Cool.

Makes 2 cups   *Margaret Taylor*

RUM FRUIT SALAD

1 cantaloupe, balled
1 honeydew melon, balled
1/8 watermelon, balled
1 cup blueberries
2/3 cup sugar
1/3 cup water
1 teaspoon lime peel, zested
6 tablespoons fresh lime juice
1/2 cup light rum
fresh mint leaves as garnish

1. Bring water and sugar to a boil. Continue boiling until reduced to a syrup. Add zested lime peel. Cool to room temperature.

2. Stir in lime juice and rum.

3. Combine melon balls. Pour syrup over fruit. Chill in refrigerator. Stir in blueberries before serving.

4. Serve chilled in an attractive bowl, garnished with fresh mint leaves.

Serves 8   *Ron and Jackie Gall*

Summer Salads

ITALIAN TOMATO AND ONION SALAD

    2   tablespoons light olive oil
    4   teaspoons balsamic vinegar
  1/8 teaspoon sugar
  1/8 teaspoon salt
  1/8 teaspoon freshly ground pepper
  1/4 cup fresh basil, julienned
    4   ounces Gorgonzola cheese, diced or crumbled
    8   fresh garden tomatoes, sliced
    2   sweet red onions, thinly sliced

1. Prepare vinaigrette by mixing together olive oil, vinegar, sugar, salt, pepper, basil and Gorgonzola. Set aside for 1 hour to allow flavors to blend.

2. Arrange sliced tomatoes and sliced onions cascaded on a large serving platter or on individual salad plates. Drizzle the vinaigrette over the top and serve.

Serves 8   *Ron and Jackie Gall*

LAYERED SPINACH SALAD

    1   (9 oz.) package cheese tortellini
    2   cups red cabbage, shredded
    6   cups spinach leaves, torn
    1   cup cherry tomatoes, halved
  1/2 cup green onion, sliced
    1   cup prepared ranch dressing
    8   slices bacon, cooked and crumbled

1. Cook tortellini to desired doneness as directed on package. Drain and rinse with cold water.

2. In a 13 x 9-inch pan layer cabbage, spinach, tortellini, tomatoes and green onion. Pour dressing evenly over top. Sprinkle with bacon. Cover and refrigerate until serving time.

Serves 8   *Marilyn Hendry*

Note: Red cabbage is only for color. Use sparingly.

Summer Salads

CURRIED CHICKEN SALAD

  2 cups chicken, cooked and cubed
  2 stalks celery, sliced
  1 ounce slivered blanched almonds
 1/2 cup golden raisins
 1-2 green onions, sliced
  1 apple, cored and cubed
   Curried Mayonnaise

1. Combine above ingredients.

2. Toss with enough Curried Mayonnaise *(See Recipe)* to moisten. Refrigerate until ready to serve.

Serves 4

CURRIED MAYONNAISE

  1 cup mayonnaise
  1 teaspoon Dijon mustard
 1/4 teaspoon salt
 1/8 teaspoon pepper
  1 tablespoon lemon juice
  1 tablespoon wine vinegar
  1 small clove garlic, minced
 1-2 teaspoons curry powder

Blend ingredients together until smooth. Chill. Use with Curried Chicken Salad *(See Recipe)*.

Makes 1 cup   *Penny Newkirk*

Summer Salads

SPINACH SALAD

1 pound fresh spinach	*Dressing:*
2 hard-cooked eggs, sliced	1 cup vegetable oil
1 red onion, thinly sliced	6 tablespoons red wine vinegar
	5 tablespoons sugar
6 strips bacon, cooked, drained and crumbled	1 teaspoon salt
	1 teaspoon dry mustard
1/2 pound fresh mushrooms, sliced	1 teaspoon onion, grated
	2 tablespoons lemon juice
	freshly ground pepper

1. Combine dressing ingredients. Shake well. Refrigerate at least 1 hour.
2. Discard spinach stems and wash leaves thoroughly. Pat dry on paper towel.
3. Combine spinach with eggs, red onion, bacon, and mushrooms.

Serves 4-6   *Judy Stratman*

GAZPACHO PASTA TOSS

1 (12 oz.) package rigatoni pasta	*Dressing:*
1 medium cucumber, sliced	3 tablespoons olive oil
1 medium green pepper, chopped	2 tablespoons fresh basil
2 tablespoons fresh parsley, chopped	2 tablespoons lemon juice
1 basket cherry tomatoes, halved	1 tablespoon red wine vinegar
1 (DR.WT. 2.5 oz.) can black olives, sliced	1/2 teaspoon salt
1 cup summer squash, sliced	1/2 teaspoon freshly ground pepper

1. Cook pasta according to package directions. Cool. Add cucumber, green pepper, parsley, tomatoes, olives and squash.
2. Mix dressing ingredients and blend well. Toss with pasta mixture and chill overnight.

Serves 6   *Carol Bushnell*

TABBOULEH SALAD

1 cup bulgur
2 cups water
1 bunch green onions, chopped
2 cloves garlic, pressed
1 cup fresh parsley, chopped
1/2 cup fresh mint leaves, chopped
1 cup prepared olive oil and vinegar dressing
juice of 1 fresh lemon
1 (15 oz.) can garbanzo beans, drained
1-2 tomatoes, sliced
2 medium cucumbers, thinly sliced

1. Combine bulgur and water in microproof container. Microwave 20 minutes, covered. Cool.

2. Combine onions, garlic, parsley, mint, dressing and lemon juice. Add cooked bulgur and garbanzo beans.

3. Refrigerate until thoroughly chilled. Serve topped with sliced tomatoes and cucumbers.

Serves 4-6   *Donna Nowatzki*

Note: This is a wonderfully refreshing salad. As a variation tomatoes and cucumbers may be chopped and stirred into tabbouleh.

Summer Salads

ROTINI PASTA SALAD

2 (16 oz.) packages tricolored rotini
2-3 carrots, peeled and shredded
1 red bell pepper, sliced
1 cup black olives, sliced

Marinade:
1 1/2 cups olive oil
1/2 cup white wine vinegar
1 teaspoon salt
1/2 teaspoon pepper
4 cloves garlic, pressed
1-2 teaspoons dried basil
1-2 teaspoons dried oregano
1 tablespoon Dijon mustard
1 tablespoon sugar

1. Cook rotini according to package directions. Drain and cool.
2. Add carrots, pepper and olives to cooked rotini in bowl.
3. In a separate bowl combine marinade ingredients. Stir well. Pour over pasta. Adjust seasonings and spices to taste.
4. Refrigerate 1-2 hours before serving to blend flavors.

Serves 8-12

Jane Briner
Persimmon Tree

Note: This was the most popular salad at the Persimmon Tree deli.

*Summer
Side Dishes*

GRILLED ANTIPASTO

1	summer squash, cubed		salt and pepper
1	zucchini, cubed	2	tablespoons balsamic vinegar
1	red onion, cut into wedges	5	tablespoons olive oil
1	yellow onion, cut into wedges	8	sun-dried tomatoes in oil
1	red pepper, cubed	1/2	cup kalamata olives, optional
1	green pepper, cubed	2	tablespoons capers, drained
10	fresh mushrooms	1	fresh lemon, cut in half and sliced
	vegetable oil		French bread slices

1. Rub fresh vegetables with vegetable oil. Add salt and pepper to taste. Microwave on full power 3-4 minutes and then skewer.

2. Grill skewered vegetables over medium high heat, 4-6 inches above coals, until golden brown. Remove from skewers and transfer to a bowl.

3. Toss vegetables with balsamic vinegar and olive oil.

4. Arrange vegetables on platter and add sun-dried tomatoes, olives, and capers. Squeeze lemon juice over vegetables. Serve with French bread slices, thinly cut and toasted.

Serves 4-6   *Ron and Jackie Gall*

SUGAR SNAP PEA, POTATO AND CHIVE SAUTE

1	pound new red potatoes, quartered	1/4	cup fresh chives, chopped
2	tablespoons olive oil		salt and freshly ground pepper
10	ounces fresh sugar snap peas, trimmed		

1. Cook potatoes in a large pot of salted boiling water just until tender. Drain.

2. Heat oil in heavy large skillet over medium heat. Add sugar snap peas and saute 2 minutes. Add potatoes and saute until heated through. Add chives and season with salt and pepper.

Serves 4   *Jan F. Kohl*

Note: Frozen sugar snap peas may be used if fresh are not available. Thaw before adding to potatoes.

GOLDEN PARMESAN POTATOES

4 large Idaho potatoes
1/4 cup flour
1/4 cup Parmesan cheese, grated
3/4 teaspoon salt
1/8 teaspoon pepper
1/2 cup butter, melted
fresh parsley, chopped

1. Preheat oven to 375°.

2. Peel potatoes and cut lengthwise into quarters. Cover with water. Combine flour, cheese, salt and pepper in a plastic bag.

3. Drain potatoes and shake in bag to coat. Arrange potatoes in a single layer in a 9 x 13-inch pan containing the melted butter.

4. Bake 60-75 minutes, turning once, or until golden brown. Garnish with parsley. Serve.

Serves 4   Penny Newkirk

SCALLOPED TOMATOES

8 medium garden fresh tomatoes, quartered
1 cup celery, chopped
1 medium onion, sliced
2 tablespoons butter
2 cloves garlic, crushed
2 tablespoons fresh cilantro, chopped
1 tablespoon fresh basil, chopped
1 teaspoon fresh oregano, chopped

Topping:
1/4 cup Parmesan cheese, grated
6 slices whole wheat bread, toasted, buttered and cubed
olive oil
salt and pepper to taste
butter

1. Preheat oven to 350°.

2. Cook celery and onion in butter until tender. Cool.

3. Add tomatoes, garlic, cilantro, basil and oregano. Place in a buttered deep dish pie plate.

4. Prepare topping: Mix cheese and bread. Add enough olive oil to bind cubes together. Add salt and pepper to taste.

5. Place topping on tomatoes. Dot with butter. Bake uncovered for 40 minutes or until topping is lightly browned.

Serves 6-8   Carol Bushnell

*Summer
Side Dishes*

BART'S BAKED BEANS

> 1 pound dried Great Northern beans
> 5 cups water
> 1 1/2 cups onion, chopped
> 1/3 cup honey
> 2 slices bacon, cut in pieces
> 1 1/2 tablespoons Dijon mustard
> 1 tablespoon tomato paste
> 2 bay leaves
> 1 clove garlic, pressed
> 2 teaspoons salt
> 1/2 teaspoon dried thyme
> brown sugar to taste

1. Rinse beans and put into heavy saucepan. Stir in remaining ingredients except brown sugar. Heat to boil. Reduce heat to simmer.

2. Simmer covered, stirring occasionally, 3 1/2-5 hours until beans are tender and have turned a rich caramel brown. If mixture is too thin, uncover saucepan during the last hour of cooking. Adjust seasonings and add brown sugar to taste. Remove bay leaves.

3. Serve immediately or refrigerate overnight. Refrigerating and reheating brings out the flavor.

Makes 5 cups *Carleen Bart*

Summer Side Dishes

EGGPLANT VERDURA

  1 medium eggplant, cut lengthwise in half, thinly sliced
  4 tomatoes, sliced
  2 tablespoons unsalted butter
  1/3 cup olive oil, divided
  1 red onion, thinly sliced
  1 yellow onion, thinly sliced
  4 medium potatoes, peeled, thinly sliced
  1 large clove garlic, minced
  3 or 4 zucchini, thinly sliced
  2 green or red peppers, seeded, cut into strips
  3 tablespoons fresh basil, chopped
  1/2 cup pitted black olives, sliced
  salt and freshly ground pepper to taste
  1 cup Parmesan cheese, grated and divided
  1/4 cup fresh parsley, chopped

1. Saute eggplant in butter and 2 tablespoons of the oil in large skillet until lightly browned.

2. Preheat oven to 375°.

3. Layer vegetables in an oiled 9 x 13-inch baking dish as follows: Half of the onions, potatoes, garlic, eggplant, zucchini, tomatoes, peppers, basil and olives. Drizzle with 3 tablespoons of the oil. Sprinkle with salt, pepper and half of the cheese. Repeat layers, omitting cheese. Heap vegetables above edge of pan as they will bake down.

4. Cover with foil and bake 35 minutes. Top with remaining cheese. Uncover and continue baking until potatoes are fork tender, about 15 minutes. Sprinkle with parsley.

Serves 8 *Mickey Lubcke*

Note: There may be more vegetables than will fit in the baking dish. Use small vegetables or be prepared to add a second casserole. This is a wonderful vegetarian main course or side dish with grilled meat.

Summer Entrees

LONDON BROIL

1 flank steak, about 2 pounds
1 tablespoon olive oil
2 teaspoons dried parsley
1 clove garlic, crushed
1 teaspoon salt
1 teaspoon lemon juice
1/2 teaspoon freshly ground pepper
   Sauteed Onions

1. Trim fat from steak. Score diagonally, 1 inch apart on both sides.
2. In a cup combine oil, parsley, garlic, salt, lemon juice and pepper. Pour over steak and marinate in refrigerator for 1-2 hours.
3. Heat barbecue grill to a high temperature.
4. Place steak on oiled grill, 4-6 inches above coals. Grill, turning frequently, for about 10-14 minutes until steak is well browned on the outside and pink inside.
5. Serve steak sliced very thinly on the diagonal, across the grain. Top each portion with Sauteed Onions *(See Recipe)*.

Serves 4-6

SAUTEED ONIONS

4 medium onions, thinly sliced
2 tablespoons butter or margarine
1/8 teaspoon paprika
1/8 teaspoon salt
2 teaspoons brown sugar

Melt butter in skillet over low heat. Add onions, paprika and salt. Cook, stirring occasionally, about 30 minutes, until onions are nicely browned. Stir in brown sugar. Cook a few minutes longer. Serve with London Broil *(See Recipe)*.

Serves 4-6 *Carol Bushnell*

Summer Entrees

TERIYAKI SEA BASS

1 cup sake or dry sherry	4 (8 oz.) sea bass fillets or swordfish steaks
3/4 cup soy sauce	green onions, chopped
1/4 cup sugar	

1. Prepare teriyaki sauce: In a small saucepan combine sake or dry sherry, soy sauce and sugar. Stir until sugar dissolves. Simmer 5 minutes and set aside.

2. Spray cold grill with nonstick cooking spray. Preheat grill or broiler to medium heat. Brush fillets with teriyaki sauce on all sides.

3. Grill fish for 3 minutes on each side. Brush again with sauce. Broil until fillets are cooked through and deep golden brown, about 1 minute per side.

4. Transfer to serving plate and sprinkle with green onions.

Serves 4   *Jan F. Kohl*

MEDITERRANEAN VEGETABLE STEW

2 tablespoons olive oil, divided	1 tablespoon red wine vinegar
1 1/4 pounds eggplant, cut into 1/2-inch cubes	1 teaspoon dried thyme
1 pound zucchini, cut into 1/2-inch cubes	1 teaspoon salt
2 pounds fresh tomatoes, peeled, seeded, chopped and divided	1/2 teaspoon freshly ground pepper
	1 (16 oz.) can garbanzo beans, drained
6 green onions, cut into 1/2-inch pieces	4 ounces feta cheese, crumbled
	couscous

1. In a Dutch oven heat 1 tablespoon olive oil. Add eggplant and cook 4 minutes, stirring often until lightly browned.

2. Add zucchini and 1 additional tablespoon olive oil. Cook 3 minutes, stirring.

3. Add green onions, vinegar, seasonings, and half of the tomatoes. Cook 5 minutes or until most of the liquid has evaporated, stirring occasionally.

4. Add garbanzo beans and remaining tomatoes. Cook 2 more minutes or until heated through.

5. To serve, remove from heat and stir in feta cheese. Spoon over prepared couscous.

Serves 4   *Ron and Jackie Gall*

Summer Entrees

BARBECUED BEEF

- 5 pounds beef chuck roast, trimmed and cut into 1-inch cubes
- 1 teaspoon salt
- 1/2 head cabbage, shredded
- 1 large yellow onion, finely chopped
- 1 green pepper, finely chopped
- 3 stalks celery, finely chopped
- 1 clove garlic, pressed
- 1 cup tomato juice
- 1 cup catsup
- 1 cup prepared barbecue sauce
- 1 cup brown sugar
- 3 tablespoons cider vinegar

1. Cover meat with water and salt. Simmer until tender. Remove meat from broth. Save broth and cool meat. When meat has cooled, shred by pulling apart.

2. To beef broth add vegetables, garlic and tomato juice. Simmer until tender. Add shredded beef, catsup and barbecue sauce. Continue cooking to reduce and thicken. When desired consistency has been reached add the brown sugar and vinegar. Adjust seasoning. Freezes well.

Serves 12   *Carol Smith*

POLYNESIAN STEAK KEBABS

- 1 1/2-2 pounds sirloin, 1-inch thick
- 3/4 cup pineapple juice
- 1/4 cup vegetable oil
- 3 tablespoons soy sauce
- 1 clove garlic, crushed
- 2 teaspoons brown sugar
- 3/4 teaspoon ground ginger
- 1 basket cherry tomatoes
- 1 large green pepper, cut into 1 1/2-inch chunks
- 12 medium mushrooms
- 2 large onions, quartered and separated

1. Trim steak of all fat and cut into 1 1/2-inch pieces. Place meat in a large bowl. Combine pineapple juice, oil, soy sauce, garlic, brown sugar and ginger. Pour over meat in bowl. Cover and refrigerate overnight.

2. Preheat outdoor grill. Remove meat from marinade and drain on paper toweling. Alternate meat and vegetables on skewers and grill 8-10 minutes on each side.

Serves 4-6   *Carol Bushnell*

Summer Entrees

MARINATED CHICKEN BREASTS

6 chicken breast halves, skinned and boned	3 cloves garlic, pressed
1/2 cup brown sugar, firmly packed	1/4 teaspoon pepper
	1 1/2 tablespoons lime juice
	1 1/2 teaspoons salt
1/3 cup olive oil	1 1/2 tablespoons lemon juice
1/4 cup cider vinegar	3 tablespoons coarse grain mustard

1. Whisk all marinade ingredients together and pour over chicken. Cover and refrigerate 2-4 hours.

2. Grill chicken breasts over hot coals for 8 minutes on each side.

3. Bring remaining marinade to a boil in a small saucepan. Cook at boil 4-5 minutes. Brush chicken with boiled marinade while grilling.

Serves 4-6

Carol Erickson

THAI-STYLE GRILLED CHICKEN

4 chicken breast halves, skinned and boned	1 tablespoon fresh ginger, grated
	1 tablespoon chili paste with garlic*
2 tablespoons lime juice	2 tablespoons fresh cilantro, chopped
2 cloves garlic, minced	4 green onions, minced
2 tablespoons fish sauce*	

1. In a bowl combine lime juice, garlic, fish sauce, ginger, chili paste and cilantro. Place the chicken breasts in the bowl and coat with marinade. Refrigerate for at least 1 hour.

2. Grill the chicken breasts for approximately 5 minutes per side.

3. Bring remaining marinade to a boil in a small saucepan. Cook at boil 4-5 minutes. Drizzle over chicken. Garnish with minced green onions and serve over rice.

Serves 4

Ron and Jackie Gall

Note: *These items are available at oriental markets or specialty food stores.

Summer Entrees

TAYLOR'S PORK SANDWICHES WITH COLESLAW

 1 *(4-5 lb.) boneless pork roast*
   vegetable oil
 2 *cloves garlic, pressed*
   freshly ground pepper
   hard rolls
   barbecue sauce
   Coleslaw Vinaigrette

1. Rub pork roast with oil, garlic and pepper. Grill over medium heat for 2-2 1/2 hours or until meat thermometer reaches 150°.
2. Cut meat in 1/4-inch slices.
3. Place 2 slices of grilled pork on a hard roll. Top with Coleslaw Vinaigrette *(See Recipe)* and barbecue sauce.

Serves 10-15   *Margaret Taylor*

Note: "A family favorite for many years."

COLESLAW VINAIGRETTE

1 *small head cabbage, shredded*	*Dressing:*
1/2 *small head red cabbage, shredded*	1 *cup vegetable oil*
4 *green onions, chopped*	1 *cup sugar*
2 *carrots, peeled and shredded*	1 *cup red wine vinegar*
1 *green pepper, chopped*	2 *teaspoons salt*
1 *red pepper, chopped*	1/4 *teaspoon pepper*
1/4 *cup fresh parsley, chopped*	

1. Combine dressing ingredients and pour over vegetables.
2. Toss well. Refrigerate 2-4 hours before serving.

Serves 8-10   *Fern Bart*
                                    Margaret Taylor

Summer Entrees

PORK IN RED CHILI SAUCE

1 1/2 pounds pork tenderloin	1/2 teaspoon salt
2 tablespoons olive oil	1/2 teaspoon dried oregano
4 tablespoons balsamic vinegar	1/2 teaspoon ground cumin
1 clove garlic, pressed	1/2 teaspoon ground cloves
1 1/2-2 tablespoons chili powder	1/4 teaspoon ground cinnamon

1. Whisk together everything but the pork and cinnamon until thoroughly blended.

2. Pour marinade over pork. Sprinkle with cinnamon and marinate in refrigerator at least 8 hours or overnight, turning occasionally.

3. Heat grill to medium high. Grill pork until center is pale pink, about 15-17 minutes. Serve immediately.

Serves 4 *Jan F. Kohl*

PASTA AND SHRIMP WITH CAPER-BASIL VINAIGRETTE

1 cup fresh basil, chopped	2 tablespoons garlic, minced
1 cup extra virgin olive oil	1 1/2 pounds fresh shrimp, peeled and deveined
1/2 cup fresh lemon juice	
1/4 cup capers	1 pound fresh linguine pasta, cooked
3 teaspoons caper juice	
1/4 cup oil-packed sun-dried tomatoes, drained and chopped	olive oil
	salt and pepper to taste

1. Whisk basil, olive oil, lemon juice, capers, caper juice, tomatoes and garlic in bowl to blend. Season with salt and pepper to taste. Let stand at room temperature at least 2 hours.

2. Prepare grill and bring to a medium high heat. Brush shrimp with olive oil and grill for 3-4 minutes turning once, until shrimp are just cooked through.

3. In large pasta bowl combine cooked pasta and shrimp. Toss with caper-basil vinaigrette. Serve immediately.

Serves 4-6 *Jan F. Kohl*

Summer Entrees

REDDENED SHRIMP

          12   (10-15 per lb.) shrimp,
                  peeled and deveined
          1/2   teaspoon salt
          2   tablespoons paprika
          1 1/2 teaspoons garlic powder
          1 1/2 teaspoons onion powder
          1 1/2 teaspoons dried basil
          1/2   teaspoon dried oregano
          1   teaspoon pepper
          1   teaspoon dried thyme
                dash cayenne pepper
                Black Bean and Rice Salsa

1. Preheat oven to 375°.
2. Mix all seasonings well in a small bowl.
3. Place shrimp and seasoning mix in a paper or food storage bag. Shake to completely coat shrimp with seasoning mix.
4. Bake shrimp on small sizzle platter for 12 minutes. Include a small amount of water to prevent sticking. Remove and serve with Black Bean and Rice Salsa (See Recipe).

Serves 2

Mary Marks, R.D., Owner
James Simmers, Executive Chef
Carvers on the Lake

Summer Entrees

BLACK BEAN AND RICE SALSA

    2 ounces olive oil
   1/2 cup scallions, chopped
   1/4 cup celery, chopped
   1/4 cup broccoli, chopped
   1/4 cup carrots, chopped
    1 teaspoon ground cumin
    1 teaspoon salt
    1 teaspoon pepper
    2 cloves garlic, crushed
    2 cups cooked brown rice
    2 cups cooked black beans
    3 ounces fresh lemon juice
    2 ounces balsamic vinegar
    2 ounces chicken broth, double strength
    6 tablespoons plain low fat yogurt
       Reddened Shrimp

1. Warm olive oil in large saute pan over high heat. Saute scallions, celery, broccoli, carrots, cumin, salt and pepper for 2 minutes.

2. Add garlic, rice and beans. Cook 1 minute. Reduce heat to medium. Add remaining ingredients except yogurt and Reddened Shrimp. Simmer about 5 minutes. Garnish each serving with 1 tablespoon yogurt. Border dish with Reddened Shrimp *(See Recipe)*.

Serves 6

Mary Marks, R.D., Owner
James Simmers, Executive Chef
Carvers on the Lake

Summer Entrees

SUMMER SPINACH TART

 2 *green onions, chopped*
 1/2 *cup fresh mushrooms, chopped*
 2 *(10 oz.) packages frozen spinach,*
   thawed and squeezed dry
 1/3 *cup light ricotta*
 1/3 *cup non fat yogurt*
 1/2 *cup Parmesan cheese, grated*
 2 *tablespoons fat free mayonnaise*
 1/8 *teaspoon dried tarragon*
  freshly grated nutmeg
 1 *(8-inch) pie crust, unbaked (optional)*

Garnish:
  cherry tomatoes, halved
  artichoke hearts, quartered
  Parmesan cheese, grated or fine bread crumbs

1. Preheat oven to 400°.
2. Saute green onions and mushrooms in a pan coated with nonstick cooking spray.
3. Add spinach, ricotta, yogurt, Parmesan, mayonnaise, tarragon and nutmeg.
4. Fill an 8-inch pie plate coated with nonstick cooking spray or pour into an 8-inch pie crust, unbaked.
5. Decorate with cherry tomato halves alternating with quartered artichoke hearts. Sprinkle with Parmesan cheese, or for a lower fat version substitute fine bread crumbs.
6. Bake 30 minutes or until golden brown.

Serves 4-6

Just Ask Jo Catering
Jo Cessna

Summer Entrees

GRILLED SWORDFISH WITH TOMATO HERB SALSA

     swordfish fillets, 1 per person
1/4 *cup olive oil*
1 *tablespoon fresh thyme, chopped*
1 *tablespoon fresh marjoram, chopped*
    Tomato Herb Salsa

Rub fillets with olive oil in which fresh herbs have been blended. Marinate in refrigerator approximately 30 minutes while grill is heating. Grill for 3-4 minutes per side or until fish flakes. Serve with Tomato Herb Salsa *(See Recipe)*.

TOMATO HERB SALSA

1/2 *teaspoon ground cumin*
1/4 *teaspoon ground coriander*
1 *cup fresh tomatoes, peeled, seeded and chopped*
2 *tablespoons red onion, chopped*
1-2 *green onions, chopped*
1 *tablespoon lime juice*
1-2 *teaspoons fresh cilantro, chopped*
    jalapeno peppers or green chilies to taste
    salt and pepper to taste

Combine all of the above ingredients and allow flavors to blend at least 1 hour. Serve with Grilled Swordfish fillets *(See Recipe)*.

Makes 1 1/2 cups   *Penny Newkirk*

Note: This salsa is also good with grilled chicken. A variation may be made by adding corn and black beans to the recipe.

Summer Entrees

MANGO SALSA

2 large ripe mangoes, cut into 1/4-inch pieces
2 green onions, chopped
zest of 1 lime plus its juice
1 jalapeno pepper, seeded and minced
1 teaspoon fresh ginger, grated
2 cloves garlic, pressed
1/3 cup fresh cilantro, chopped

1. Combine all ingredients and refrigerate for 1 hour.
2. Serve as a condiment to grilled swordfish or other meaty fish.

Makes 2 1/2 cups   Jan F. Kohl

PITAKEY SANDWICHES

1-2 cloves garlic, pressed
5-6 medium zucchini, thinly sliced
2 medium onions, sliced
2 tablespoons olive oil
8 ounces Cheddar cheese, shredded
fresh alfalfa sprouts
4 pita bread rounds
1/2 cup mayonnaise
1 tablespoon Dijon mustard

1. Cut pita bread rounds in half and open pocket.
2. Saute garlic, zucchini and onions in olive oil until tender.
3. Mix mayonnaise and mustard together and spread inside pita half. Add hot zucchini mixture. Top with cheese and sprouts.

Serves 4   Kerry Bart-Raber

Note: This is a really great use for summer zucchini.

Summer Entrees

ZUCCHINI QUICHE

1 (9-inch) deep dish pie shell, baked and cooled	1/8 teaspoon pepper
2 tablespoons margarine	3 medium zucchini, cut into 1/8-inch slices
2 cloves garlic, pressed	3/4 pound Monterey Jack cheese, cubed
1/4 teaspoon salt	3 eggs, lightly beaten
1/4 teaspoon dried dill	1 cup unsalted cashews

1. Preheat oven to 325°.
2. Melt margarine. Add garlic and zucchini. Saute until limp, stirring often. Add seasonings.
3. Line pie shell with cashews. Add zucchini and cheese. Pour eggs over the top.
4. Bake 45 minutes.

Serves 4-6   *Judy Stratman*

Note: "This is Grandma's favorite dish."

SUMMER TOMATO SAUCE WITH LINGUINE

4 large vine ripened tomatoes, cut into 1/2-inch cubes	1 cup extra virgin olive oil
1 pound Brie cheese, rind removed, torn into irregular pieces (or 1 can anchovies, drained and chopped)	3 garlic cloves, pressed
	1/2 teaspoon salt
	1/2 teaspoon freshly ground pepper
	Parmesan cheese, freshly grated
1 cup fresh basil, coarsely chopped	1 1/2 pounds linguine pasta

1. Prepare dressing at least 2 hours, but no longer than 1 day, before serving. Combine tomatoes, Brie (or anchovies), basil, garlic, olive oil, salt and pepper in a large serving bowl. Cover and set aside at room temperature, stirring occasionally.
2. Cook pasta according to package directions. Drain and immediately toss with the tomato sauce. Serve at once, passing the pepper mill and Parmesan cheese.

Serves 4-6   *Jan F. Kohl*

Note: Make this sauce only with vine ripened summer tomatoes.

Summer Entrees

PASTA AND VEGETABLES

    2 tablespoons olive oil
    1 clove garlic, pressed
    1 small onion, cut into wedges
  1/2 cup fresh broccoli, chopped
  1/2 cup fresh cauliflower, chopped
    1 tomato, cut into wedges
    2 cups of any combination of the following:
          carrots, cut into strips
          fresh mushrooms, sliced
          zucchini, sliced
          summer squash, sliced
          green pepper strips
       red pepper flakes to taste
       salt and pepper to taste
  3/4 pound thin spaghetti, cooked
       Parmesan cheese, grated

1. Heat oil in skillet or wok. Add garlic. Stir-fry all vegetables except tomato until hot and slightly tender. Add tomato, red pepper flakes, salt and pepper. Heat through.

2. Serve over pasta. Top with Parmesan cheese.

Serves 4   *Maggie Burmeister*

FRESH HERB PASTA SAUCE

1/2 cup fresh herbs (chives, parsley, thyme, savory, oregano or basil)	1/2 cup olive oil
	2-3 cloves garlic, minced
	1 pound pasta, cooked
1 stick butter	Parmesan cheese, freshly grated

1. Chop a mixture of fresh, cleaned and dried herbs. In saute pan melt butter. Add olive oil and garlic. Heat.

2. Add chopped herbs and toss with pasta. Serve with Parmesan cheese.

Serves 4-6   *Penny Newkirk*

Summer Entrees

PESTO SAUCE FOR PASTA

- 1/4 cup pine nuts
- 2 cups fresh basil leaves, packed
- 1/8 teaspoon pepper
- 1/2 cup Parmesan cheese, freshly grated
- 2 large cloves garlic, minced
- 1/2 cup olive oil

1. In food processor bowl process well-dried basil leaves, pepper, garlic and pine nuts.
2. While machine is running gradually add olive oil to form an emulsion.
3. Add Parmesan cheese. Thin with additional oil if needed. Freezes well with a thin layer of olive oil covering the surface.

Serving Suggestions:

1. Dip: 2 tablespoons of pesto with 1/2 cup mayonnaise and 1 cup sour cream. Great with fresh vegetables or as a spread on sandwiches.
2. Marinade: 6 tablespoons pesto plus 1/3 cup red wine vinegar and 2/3 cup additional olive oil. Use over sliced fresh tomatoes, as a salad dressing or with steamed fresh mushrooms for antipasto.
3. Sauce: Thin pesto with additional olive oil and serve over hot pasta.

Makes 1-1 1/2 cups

Roberta Sprowl
Penny Newkirk

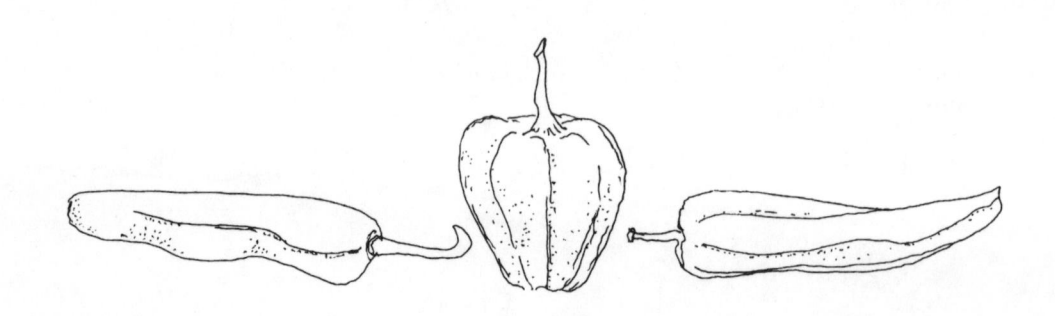

SYMPHONY TEA BARS

    1 cup butter
    2 cups sugar
    4 eggs
  1/2 teaspoon vanilla
    2 cups flour
  1/2 teaspoon salt
    2 cups pecans, chopped
    2 ounces unsweetened chocolate, melted

Frosting:
    5 tablespoons flour
    1 cup milk
    1 cup butter
    1 cup sugar
    2 teaspoons vanilla

1. Preheat oven to 350°. Grease a 9 x 13-inch pan.

2. Cream butter and sugar until fluffy. Add eggs and vanilla. Beat well. Add flour, salt, and pecans.

3. Put half of the batter in baking pan. Add melted chocolate to the remaining batter and spread over batter in pan. Bake 30 minutes. Cool.

4. *Frosting:* In top of double boiler blend flour and milk. Cook over low heat, stirring constantly until a paste is formed. Cool. Cream together butter, sugar and vanilla. Add paste mixture and beat 5 minutes.

5. Spread frosting over cooled bars.

Makes 20 bars   *Carol Juntunen*

Note: Take these very rich bars to the symphony picnic for an extra special treat.

Summer Desserts

PICNIC CHOCOLATE CAKE

- 1/2 cup butter
- 2 1/4 cups brown sugar, packed
- 2 eggs
- 2 (1 oz.) squares unsweetened chocolate, melted
- 1/2 cup buttermilk
- 2 teaspoons vanilla
- 1 cup boiling water
- 2 teaspoons baking soda
- 2 1/4 cups flour

Frosting:
- 3 tablespoons unsweetened cocoa
- 1/2 cup butter
- 6 tablespoons milk
- 3 1/2 cups powdered sugar
- 1 teaspoon vanilla
- 1 cup nuts, chopped

1. Preheat oven to 400°. Grease an 11 x 15-inch jelly roll pan.

2. Cream butter and brown sugar. Add eggs and beat until fluffy. Stir in chocolate, buttermilk, vanilla and water mixed with baking soda. Blend in flour. Pour into prepared pan.

3. Bake 20 minutes or until toothpick inserted into center comes out clean.

4. Prepare frosting: In a saucepan bring to a boil the cocoa, butter and milk. Add powdered sugar, vanilla and nuts. Mix well. Immediately spread on warm cake.

Makes 24 pieces

Donna Andrini
Shirley Yuill

Summer Desserts

LIGHT-AS-AIR SPONGE CAKE

6 eggs, separated	1 1/2 cups cake flour, sifted
1/2 cup cold water	1/4 teaspoon salt
1 1/2 cups sugar	3/4 teaspoon cream of tartar
1 teaspoon vanilla	

1. Preheat oven to 350°.
2. Beat egg yolks until thick and lemon colored. Add water and continue beating until thick (about 5 minutes).
3. Add sugar and vanilla. Beat well.
4. Fold in flour with salt, a small amount at a time.
5. In a separate bowl beat egg whites with cream of tartar until stiff. Fold into egg yolk mixture.
6. Put mixture into ungreased angel food cake pan. Bake 55-60 minutes.
7. Remove from oven and invert pan on funnel to cool. When completely cooled remove from pan.

Serves 12   *Olga Newkirk*

DELI-STYLE CHEESECAKE

2 cups nonfat cottage cheese	1/4 cup fresh lemon juice
2 tablespoons low fat margarine, melted	1 tablespoon lemon zest
1/2 cup egg substitute	**Crust:**
1/2 cup sugar	1 1/4 cups graham cracker crumbs
1/2 cup evaporated skim milk	1/4 cup sugar
1/4 cup flour	1/3 cup low fat margarine

1. Preheat oven to 300°.
2. Prepare crust: Combine graham cracker crumbs, sugar and margarine. Press into an 8 1/2-inch springform pan.
3. In food processor blend the cottage cheese until creamy. Add margarine, egg substitute, sugar, evaporated milk, flour, lemon juice and lemon zest. Blend well. Pour into pan.
4. Bake 1 1/2 hours or until set in center when tested. Cool several hours before serving.

Serves 10   *Kathy Blomquist*

Summer Desserts

LEMONADE PIE

1 graham cracker crust, baked
1 (6 oz.) can frozen lemonade concentrate, thawed
1 (14 oz.) can sweetened condensed milk
12 ounces frozen whipped topping, thawed

1. Mix lemonade concentrate and condensed milk. Fold in whipped topping.
2. Pour into crust. Freeze covered.

Serves 6   Joyce Currie

FRESH STRAWBERRY-LEMON PIE

2 quarts fresh strawberries, sliced and divided
1 cup sugar
3 tablespoons cornstarch
3/4 cup water
2 teaspoons lemon zest
1 tablespoon fresh lemon juice

Graham Cracker Crust:
1 1/4 cups graham cracker crumbs
1/3 cup butter
1/4 cup sugar
1 tablespoon lemon zest

whipped cream

1. Preheat oven to 350°.
2. Prepare crust: Melt butter. Add sugar, graham cracker crumbs and lemon zest. Press mixture firmly in bottom and up sides of 9-inch pie pan. Bake 8-10 minutes. Cool.
3. Puree 1 quart of strawberries to make 2 cups of puree. Combine sugar and cornstarch in saucepan. Add water and strawberry puree. Simmer, stirring constantly until thickened. Remove from heat. Add lemon juice and lemon zest. Cool slightly. Pour over remaining sliced berries in prepared pie shell. Refrigerate until serving time.
4. Serve garnished with whipped cream.

Serves 6-8   Carleen Bart

Summer Desserts

MARGARITA PIE

1 1/2 cans sweetened condensed milk
2/3 cup lime juice
4 1/2 tablespoons tequila
4 1/2 tablespoons Triple Sec
3/4 cup frozen strawberries in syrup, thawed
3/4 cup heavy cream, whipped
1 (9-inch) graham cracker crust, baked

1. Combine condensed milk, lime juice, tequila and Triple Sec. Stir in strawberries and syrup.

2. Fold in whipped cream.

3. Pour into prepared crust. Cover and refrigerate 3-4 hours to set.

Serves 6-8

Kelly Phelps
the Hill Street Bed and Breakfast

the
Hill
Street

Bed
and
Breakfast

Summer Desserts

TURTLE PIE

1 1/2 cups chocolate wafers, crushed
2 tablespoons butter, melted
1 cup marshmallows
1 1/4 cups evaporated milk
1/2 gallon vanilla or
     butter pecan ice cream, softened
1 cup semi-sweet chocolate chips
1/2 cup caramel topping
    whipped cream
    pecan halves

1. Combine crushed wafers and butter. Press into a 10-inch pie plate.

2. Melt marshmallows and chocolate chips with milk. Cook over medium heat until mixture coats a spoon. Cool.

3. Place half of the ice cream in crust and freeze. Then layer cooled chocolate mixture, the remaining ice cream and the caramel topping, freezing after each layer is added.

4. Remove pie from freezer and let it sit at room temperature for 15 minutes before serving. Garnish with whipped cream and pecan halves.

Serves 12   *Carol Juntunen*

KEY LIME PIE

1 (8-inch) graham cracker crust, baked
1 can sweetened condensed milk
1/2 cup Key West lime juice
3 drops green food coloring
8 ounces frozen whipped topping, thawed and divided

1. Combine condensed milk, lime juice, food coloring and 6 ounces whipped topping.

2. Pour into prepared pie crust. Top with remaining 2 ounces whipped topping. Chill several hours before serving.

Serves 6-8   *Jean McPartlin*

Note: This pie is excellent, fast, easy and delicious!

*Summer
Desserts*

CHOCOLATE PEANUT BUTTER PIE

   1 graham cracker crust, baked
   1 (3 oz.) package instant chocolate pudding
1 1/2 cups cold milk
   1 (8 oz.) package cream cheese, softened
2/3 cup sugar
1/2 cup peanut butter
   8 ounces frozen whipped topping, thawed and divided

1. Mix pudding with cold milk and beat. Pour into crust. Chill.

2. Beat together cream cheese, sugar, and peanut butter until light. Fold in half of the whipped topping. Spread over the pudding layer.

3. Cover with remaining whipped topping. Chill until firm.

Serves 8-10   *Lisa Herrera*

EMMA'S SCHAUM TORTE

   6 large egg whites
1 1/2 cups sugar
3/4 teaspoon cream of tartar
   1 teaspoon vanilla
   1 tablespoon vinegar
   1 pint vanilla ice cream
   1 quart fresh raspberries

1. Preheat oven to 500°.

2. Beat egg whites and cream of tartar until stiff. Gradually add sugar, vanilla and vinegar.

3. Grease the bottom of a springform pan and place egg white mixture into pan. Bake for 10 minutes. Turn off oven and let sit overnight.

4. Place torte on a serving plate. Fill center with vanilla ice cream. Spoon fresh berries over the top.

Serves 8   *Emma Michels*

Summer Desserts

RAINBOW SHERBET MACAROON

  4 egg whites
  1 teaspoon vanilla
  1 1/3 cups sugar
  2 1/2 cups flaked coconut
  12 ounces light frozen whipped topping, thawed
  3 tablespoons sugar
  1/2-1 cup slivered almonds, toasted
  3 quarts sherbet, 3 different flavors

1. Preheat oven to 325°.

2. Beat egg whites and vanilla until soft peaks form. Gradually add sugar, beating until stiff. Fold in coconut.

3. Drop by large spoonfuls onto greased nonstick cookie sheet.

4. Bake 25 minutes or until lightly browned. Cool and then crumble.

5. Combine whipped topping, sugar, macaroon crumbs and almonds.

6. Spread one-third of mixture into a 9 x 13-inch pan. Spoon sherbet over this layer, varying colors. Add remaining whipped cream mixture and freeze.

7. To serve: Spoon into ice cream dishes or cut into squares.

Serves 12-15   *Carleen Bart*

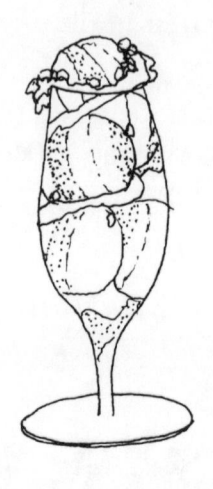

Autumn

Table of Contents

Appetizers
Breads
Soups
Salads
Side Dishes
Entrees
Desserts

Autumn Appetizers

CHEESE-STUFFED SURULLITOS

2 cups water	5 ounces extra sharp Cheddar cheese
1 teaspoon salt	vegetable oil
1 1/2 cups cornmeal	salsa
1 (4.5 oz.) can chopped green chilies	

1. Boil water and salt. Gradually add cornmeal, stirring vigorously over medium heat until mixture forms a ball and pulls away from sides of pan. Remove from heat. Stir in chilies. Cool.

2. Preheat oven to 350°.

3. Cut cheese into 1/4-inch by 2-inch sticks. Shape 2 tablespoons of dough around cheese. Press dough tightly around cheese to seal.

4. Brush lightly with oil and bake for 15 minutes until cheese is melted. Cool to room temperature and serve with salsa for dipping.

Makes 20 appetizers *Karen Gimse*

MEXICAN DIP

3 ripe avocados	1 (10 oz.) can bean dip
2 teaspoons lemon juice	1 bunch green onions, finely chopped
1/2 teaspoon salt	
1/2 teaspoon pepper	8 ounces Cheddar cheese, grated
1 cup sour cream	2 fresh tomatoes, chopped
1/2 cup mayonnaise	1 (6 oz.) can chopped black olives, drained
1 package taco seasoning mix	

1. Peel, pit and mash avocados. Add lemon juice, salt and pepper.

2. Combine sour cream, mayonnaise and taco seasoning.

3. To assemble: Spread bean dip on a large platter. Cover with avocado mixture. Top with sour cream mixture. Sprinkle with green onions, cheese, tomatoes, and olives. Serve at room temperature with tortilla chips.

Serves 12 *Marla Olson*

Autumn Appetizers

PITA CHIPS

- 1 (14 oz.) package pita bread
- 1/2 cup olive oil
- 1 clove garlic, minced
- fresh herbs (dill, oregano and rosemary), chopped
- salt and pepper to taste
- 1/3 cup Parmesan cheese, grated
- sesame or poppy seed, optional

1. Preheat oven to 350°.
2. In large bowl whisk together olive oil, garlic, fresh herbs, salt and pepper.
3. Open each pita into a single round. Brush each circle on both sides with oil mixture. Cut each circle into 6 wedges.
4. Place on an ungreased baking sheet. Sprinkle with salt, Parmesan cheese and sesame or poppy seed, if desired.
5. Bake for 10 minutes. Turn and bake for an additional 8 minutes, or until crisp and golden. Serve warm or at room temperature with dips and spreads. Serve with Black Bean Hummus *(See Recipe)*.

Makes lots of chips

BLACK BEAN HUMMUS

- 1 (15 oz.) can black beans, drained
- 2 (15 oz.) cans garbanzo beans, drained
- 8 ounces sesame tahini paste
- 1 tablespoon garlic, minced
- 1/4 cup fresh lemon juice
- 2 tablespoons salt
- 3/4 to 1 cup water
- cayenne pepper or hot sauce to taste
- tomato salsa
- Pita Chips

1. In bowl of food processor puree drained beans, tahini paste, garlic, lemon juice, salt and enough water to form a paste-like dip. Process until smooth consistency. Add cayenne or hot sauce to taste. Refrigerate to blend flavors.
2. To serve: Mound in shallow bowl and garnish with salsa. Serve with Pita Chips *(See Recipe)* for dipping.

Makes 3 cups

Ron and Jackie Gall

Autumn Breads

CORNMEAL SOUR CREAM BISCUITS

1 cup flour	1/2 teaspoon salt
1 cup cornmeal	4 tablespoons margarine
1 tablespoon sugar	3/4 cup sour cream
1 1/2 teaspoons baking powder	1/4 cup milk
1 teaspoon baking soda	

1. Preheat oven to 425°. Combine dry ingredients and stir well. Cut in margarine with pastry blender.

2. Combine sour cream and milk. Add liquid to dry ingredients all at once. Stir only until dough sticks together.

3. Turn dough onto floured board. Fold over and flatten 6 times. Pat dough to 3/4-inch thickness. Cut out biscuits and place on greased baking sheet. Bake 15 minutes until lightly browned.

Makes 12 biscuits   *Eric Bart*

BUSY DAY BISCUITS

1 package dry yeast	1 teaspoon baking soda
1/4 cup warm water (110°)	1 teaspoon salt
2 cups buttermilk	1/4 cup sugar
5 cups all-purpose flour	1 cup margarine
1 tablespoon baking powder	

1. Combine yeast and water. Let stand 5 minutes to dissolve yeast. Add buttermilk to yeast mixture and set aside.

2. Combine flour, baking powder, baking soda, salt and sugar. Cut in margarine with a pastry blender. Add buttermilk mixture, stirring ingredients until well blended. Knead dough 5 times by flattening with fingertips and folding over itself into thirds, folding in an opposite direction each time. The dough may be stored in a plastic bag for up to 1 week in the refrigerator.

3. To bake: Preheat oven to 400°. Roll out dough to 1/2-inch thickness on a lightly floured surface. Cut biscuits with biscuit cutter. Bake on lightly greased baking sheet for 15-20 minutes.

Makes 3-4 dozen biscuits   *Joanne Cooke, M.S., R.D.*

Note: The texture of these wonderful biscuits is similar to refrigerated rolled dough crescent rolls. The recipe would be excellent baked as 1 large biscuit to use for a sandwich base or as a crust for appetizers.

Autumn Breads

CRANBERRY BREAD

2	cups flour
1/2	teaspoon salt
1 1/2	teaspoons baking powder
1/2	teaspoon baking soda
1	cup sugar
1	egg, beaten
2	tablespoons butter, melted
1/2	cup plus 1 1/2 tablespoons orange juice
2	tablespoons hot water
1/2	cup nuts, chopped
1	cup fresh cranberries
	rind of 1 orange, grated

1. Preheat oven to 350°.

2. Blend together flour, salt, baking powder, baking soda and sugar. In a separate bowl combine egg, butter, orange juice and water. Stir liquid ingredients into dry ingredients only until evenly moistened. Stir in cranberries, nuts and orange rind. Turn dough into greased and floured loaf pan.

3. Bake 60-70 minutes until toothpick inserted in center comes out clean. Let loaf sit in pan 10 minutes before loosening sides and removing it from pan to cooling rack. Freezes well.

Makes 1 loaf *Carol Erickson*

Note: "The holidays aren't the same without this bread. I used to help my grandmother make it."

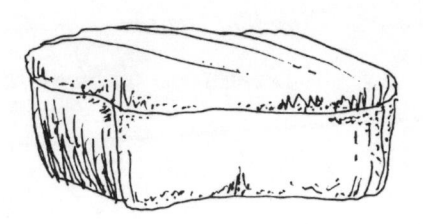

Autumn Soups

APPLE BRIE SOUP

   1   quart heavy whipping cream
   2   cups apple cider
   1   teaspoon ground cinnamon
   1   teaspoon ground nutmeg
   1   cup white wine
 1/2 cup brandy
 1/2 cup sugar
   1   (8 oz.) wheel Brie cheese
 1/4 cup roux (See Note)

1. In heavy saucepan, heat cream and cider to just below a boil. Add sugar, nutmeg and cinnamon. Simmer 5 minutes. Add wine and brandy, simmering 10 minutes longer.

2. Meanwhile, puree Brie cheese in food processor (rind and all) until creamy.

3. Whip cheese into warm cream and wine mixture. DO NOT BOIL.

4. Whip in roux with a wire whisk and cook at very low simmer 5 additional minutes.

Makes 2 quarts   *James Simmers,*
                                                               Executive Chef
                                                               Carvers on the Lake

Note: To make a roux for thickening soups and sauces, mix equal parts of melted butter and flour. Drop by measured tablespoon onto baking sheet and freeze. Keep in a plastic bag for use when needed.

This soup is a favorite at the Green Lake Golden Days Harvest Festival held each year in September.

Autumn Soups

CREAM OF CELERY SOUP WITH STILTON

> 6 tablespoons butter or margarine
> 4 cups (1 pound) celery, chopped
> 1 1/2 cups onion or leek, chopped
> pinch of sugar
> 1 cup raw rice, cooked
> 6 cups chicken broth
> 1 cup half-and-half
> salt and pepper to taste
> 2-3 ounces Stilton cheese, crumbled

1. Melt butter or margarine in stockpot. Stir in celery, onion or leek and pinch of sugar (this helps to faster break down the celery fiber). Saute until the vegetables are tender.
2. Puree rice and vegetables with broth in food processor. (If a chunky soup is desired do not puree all the celery mixture.) Return to stockpot.
3. Add half-and-half, salt, pepper and Stilton cheese. Simmer (never boil) until serving time.

Serves 8-10   *Penny Newkirk*

Note: "I tasted this combination in a pub in Ludlow, England. I came home and created my own version. Great for an English tea."

SWEET POTATO SOUP

> 3-4 sweet potatoes, cooked and peeled
> 3 cups beef broth
> 3 cups chicken broth
> 1/2 cup heavy cream
> 1/2 cup Swiss cheese, grated
> 2 tablespoons butter
> salt and white pepper to taste
> nutmeg, freshly grated

1. Puree sweet potatoes in food processor with enough broth to blend smoothly. Place in stockpot or Dutch oven with remaining broth and cream. Simmer 45 minutes to 1 hour.
2. Skim soup if foamy. Whisk in butter and grated cheese. Stir until cheese melts. Add salt, pepper and nutmeg.

Serves 8   *Penny Newkirk*

Note: Wonderful as a first course soup for luncheon. Even people who don't care for sweet potatoes like this soup.

Autumn Soups

PENNSYLVANIA DUTCH CHICKEN CORN SOUP

1	large onion, chopped
3-4	ribs celery, thinly sliced
2-3	carrots, thinly sliced
6	ears fresh corn
2-3	cups chicken, cooked and diced
	salt and pepper to taste
1/2	teaspoon thyme
4	quarts homemade chicken stock, degreased
	Spaetzle
2	hard-cooked eggs, chopped

1. Warm chicken stock. Add seasonings and prepared vegetables, except corn. Cook 30-45 minutes to blend flavors and soften vegetables.

2. While soup cooks blanch corn for 5 minutes in boiling water and cut kernels from cobs. Set aside.

3. Add corn kernels and chicken. Adjust seasonings. Simmer while making Spaetzle *(See Recipe)*. To serve: Add Spaetzle and garnish soup with hard-cooked eggs.

Serves 10-12

SPAETZLE (German Dumplings)

2	eggs
2	cups flour
2/3	cup milk
	soup stock

1. Beat eggs and add flour and milk, alternately. Beat until smooth.

2. Over boiling soup stock place spaetzle maker or make dumplings by cutting small pieces of dough and dropping them into stock. They will rise to the surface as they are cooked.

Serves 10-12 *Olga Newkirk*

NEW ENGLAND CLAM CHOWDER

>   3   (6 oz.) cans minced clams,   1/2   cup flour
>   drained and liquid reserved   1   cup clam juice
>   3-4 ribs celery, chopped   2   cups milk
>   1   small onion, chopped   2   cups half-and-half
>   2   carrots, chopped   1/4   teaspoon dried thyme
>   3   medium potatoes, peeled and diced 1 small bay leaf, cracked
>   1/2 cup margarine   white pepper to taste

1. Cook potatoes in 1 cup clam juice until tender and set aside.

2. Melt margarine in stockpot. Saute onion, celery and carrots. Add flour and blend until flour has no remaining lumps.

3. Add cooked potatoes and their liquid to stockpot. Add clam juice from drained clams. Blend in milk and half-and-half. Add seasonings.

4. Simmer (never boil cream soups) approximately 30-40 minutes. Before serving time add minced clams just to heat through. Remove bay leaf. Taste and adjust seasonings as needed.

Serves 6-8   *Penny Newkirk*

TAILGATE PUMPKIN SOUP

>   2   tablespoons margarine   1   cup canned pumpkin
>   1/2 cup onion,   1/2 cup white wine
>   finely chopped   1   teaspoon sugar
>   1   clove garlic, minced   3/4 teaspoon salt
>   1/2 cup celery, chopped   1/4 teaspoon ground cinnamon
>   3   cups chicken broth   1/8 teaspoon ground allspice

1. Melt margarine and add onion, garlic and celery. Saute for 3 minutes.

2. Add remaining ingredients. Simmer, stirring occasionally, for 30 minutes.

3. Puree mixture in blender or in food processor.

4. Cover. Refrigerate for 24 hours. Reheat or serve chilled.

Serves 6   *Roberta Sprowl*

Autumn Salads

CASHEW SALAD WITH POPPY SEED DRESSING

- 1 cup cashew nuts, chopped
- 2 cups unpeeled red apples, chopped
- 1 cup Swiss cheese, grated
- Assorted greens: iceberg, romaine, spinach, red and green leaf lettuce

Dressing:
- 1/2 cup sugar
- 1/3 cup red wine vinegar
- 2 tablespoons poppy seed
- 1 cup vegetable oil
- 1 tablespoon onion, grated
- 1/2 teaspoon salt

1. Wash and tear greens. Refrigerate.

2. Prepare dressing: In food processor combine sugar, vinegar, onion and salt. With machine running, slowly add oil. Stir in poppy seed. Refrigerate dressing.

3. Toss greens with cashews, apples, Swiss cheese and dressing immediately before serving.

Serves 4-6   *Lisa Herrera*

PINEAPPLE SALAD

- 1/2 cup sugar
- 1 tablespoon cornstarch
- 1 teaspoon cider vinegar
- 1 egg
- 1 (16 oz.) can crushed pineapple, drained
- 1 cup unsalted peanuts, chopped
- 8 ounces frozen whipped topping, thawed
- 4 large unpeeled Granny Smith apples, diced

1. The day before serving combine sugar and cornstarch in saucepan. Add vinegar, egg and pineapple. Cook over low heat until thick, stirring constantly. Refrigerate overnight.

2. To serve: Combine sauce with whipped topping. Stir in peanuts and apples.

Serves 6-8   *Diane Olsen*

Note: This is a good Thanksgiving salad.

Autumn Salads

ULTIMATE SALAD

    1   large clove garlic, pressed
  2 1/2 tablespoons vegetable oil
  2-3 tomatoes, seeded and chopped
  1 1/2 heads romaine lettuce, torn into bite size pieces
    6 green onions, chopped
  1/2 cup Romano cheese, grated
  1/4 pound bacon, cooked, drained and crumbled

Dressing:
    1 tablespoon Dijon mustard
  1/3 cup vegetable oil
      juice of 1 lemon
  1/2 teaspoon dried oregano
      salt and pepper to taste

1. Layer salad ingredients in order given above. Refrigerate until ready to serve. Prepare at least 8 hours before serving.

2. Mix dressing ingredients. Toss with salad just before serving.

Serves 4-6   *Carole Clark*

CRANBERRY RELISH

    2 pounds fresh cranberries
    3 apples, peeled, cored and diced
    2 pears, peeled, cored and diced
    2 cups golden raisins
    2 cups sugar
    1 cup fresh orange juice
    2 tablespoons orange peel, grated
    2 teaspoons ground cinnamon
  1/4 teaspoon ground nutmeg
  1/2 cup orange flavored liqueur

1. Heat all ingredients except liqueur to boiling. Reduce heat and simmer uncovered, stirring frequently until mixture thickens, about 45 minutes. Cool slightly and add liqueur.

2. Refrigerate, covered, 4 hours or overnight.

Makes 8 cups   *Mickey Lubcke*

*Autumn
Side Dishes*

CORN PUDDING

1 pound frozen corn	2 tablespoons flour
1 small green pepper, chopped	3 tablespoons sugar
1 (2 oz.) jar pimento, chopped	3 tablespoons butter, melted
1/3 pound American cheese, diced	3/4 teaspoon salt
3 eggs, beaten	3/4 cup milk

1. Preheat oven to 350°.

2. Combine together all of the above ingredients in a large mixing bowl.

3. Pour into a greased 1 1/2-quart baking dish. Bake uncovered for 60-90 minutes or until knife inserted into center comes out clean.

Serves 6-8   *Justin Bart*

Note: Baking time varies with depth of casserole.

CARROTS LYONNAISE

1 pound carrots, peeled and julienned
2 tablespoons margarine
1 small green pepper, sliced and julienned
1 medium onion, sliced
2 tablespoons brown sugar
1/4 teaspoon salt
 dash pepper
2 tablespoons chicken broth
1 teaspoon cornstarch

1. Precook carrots to crisp-tender. Do not overcook. May be done ahead of time.

2. Melt margarine. Add green pepper and onion. Saute until softened. Add carrots and saute until heated.

3. Dissolve cornstarch in chicken broth. Add to carrots with brown sugar, salt and pepper. Cook slowly, stirring constantly, until vegetables are tender, liquid has evaporated and carrots are nicely glazed.

Serves 4-6   *Elizabeth Michaelsen*

*Autumn
Side Dishes*

HARVEST CARROTS

4 cups carrots, sliced,
   cooked and drained
1 medium onion, chopped
2 tablespoons butter, melted
1 (10 3/4 oz.) can cream of celery soup
1 cup Cheddar cheese, shredded

Topping:
1 1/2 cups herb seasoned
   stuffing mix, crushed
1/4 cup butter, melted

1. Preheat oven to 350°.

2. Saute onion in butter. Cool. Add soup, carrots and cheese. Place in a 9 x 9-inch casserole.

3. For topping: Mix stuffing mix and butter together. Sprinkle mixture on top of casserole.

4. Bake 30-40 minutes until hot and bubbly.

Serves 4-6   *Carol Ludemann*

SCALLOPED MUSHROOMS

3 pounds fresh mushrooms, halved
8 whole mushroom caps for top
1/2 cup butter
1 cup heavy cream
1/2 teaspoon salt
1/2 teaspoon pepper
1/8 teaspoon cayenne pepper
3 cups Monterey Jack cheese, shredded

1. Preheat oven to 400°.

2. In 2 large frying pans, saute mushroom halves in butter over medium heat. Add cream and continue to cook until liquid is almost gone, stirring as needed. Add seasonings.

3. Scoop into a 2-quart casserole. Cover with shredded cheese and garnish with mushroom caps.

4. Bake about 10 minutes, until cheese is melted and lightly browned.

Serves 12   *Marlene McPartlin*
Julie McPartlin

Note: Very rich and good. Excellent with beef or poultry.

Autumn Side Dishes

SWEET-AND-SOUR RED CABBAGE

    1   medium head red cabbage, shredded
    4   slices bacon

Dressing:

         bacon drippings
  1/2 cup brown sugar
  3-4 tablespoons flour
  1/2 cup vinegar
  1/2 cup water

1. Cover and simmer cabbage for 35-40 minutes until tender.

2. Fry bacon until crisp. Drain and crumble. Add sugar, flour, vinegar and water to bacon drippings. Stir to blend. Cook until thickened.

3. Pour sauce over cooked cabbage. Blend.

Serves 6-8   *Olga Newkirk*

Note: This is a traditional Pennsylvania Dutch recipe from the Amish in York, Pennsylvania. Delicious served with roasted pork.

DANISH CREAM GARLIC POTATOES

    8   medium potatoes, peeled and sliced
         nutmeg, freshly grated
  2-3 cloves garlic, pressed
         salt and pepper
  24 ounces whipping cream
    2   cups mozzarella cheese, shredded

1. Preheat oven to 350°. Grease a 9 x 13-inch pan with nonstick cooking spray.

2. Layer potatoes with nutmeg, garlic, salt and pepper. Pour whipping cream over potatoes. Bake 1 1/4 hours.

3. Cover potatoes with mozzarella cheese. Bake an additional 15 minutes more.

Serves 8   *Diane Olsen*

*Autumn
Side Dishes*

FRENCH ROASTED POTATOES

24	small unpeeled red potatoes, quartered
4-5	cloves garlic, minced
3	tablespoons margarine, melted and divided
3-4	tablespoons Dijon mustard
1/2	cup fresh parsley, chopped
1/4	teaspoon freshly ground pepper
	salt to taste

1. Preheat oven to 375°.

2. Place potatoes, garlic and 2 tablespoons of margarine in a 9 x 13-inch pan. Cover with foil and bake 45-60 minutes, stirring occasionally.

3. Blend mustard, 1 tablespoon margarine, parsley, salt and pepper. Toss with potatoes to coat. Bake uncovered for 15 minutes.

Serves 8 *Diane Olsen*

SHERRIED SWEET POTATOES

8	medium sweet potatoes, baked and skinned	1/3	cup sherry
		1	teaspoon salt
2	cups orange juice		zest of 1 orange
2	tablespoons cornstarch	1/2	cup light raisins
1/3	cup butter	1/4	cup walnuts, chopped
1	cup brown sugar		

1. Preheat oven to 325°.

2. Cut potatoes lengthwise into 1/2-inch slices. Place in a buttered 9 x 13-inch baking dish.

3. Combine orange juice with cornstarch. Blend until smooth. Add butter, brown sugar, sherry, salt and orange zest. Simmer, stirring constantly, until thick and clear. Add raisins and walnuts.

4. Pour hot mixture over potatoes and bake for 30 minutes until bubbly.

Serves 8 *Margaret Kalte*

*Autumn
Side Dishes*

GOAT CHEESE MASHED POTATOES

2 pounds yellow-fleshed potatoes
6 cloves garlic, peeled
1/3 cup heavy cream
1/2 cup unsalted butter
6-9 ounces Montrachet goat cheese
1/4 cup green onion, minced
salt and pepper to taste

1. Peel the potatoes and cut into 2-inch pieces. In a large saucepan combine the potatoes and the garlic cloves. Add enough cold salted water to cover the potatoes plus 1/2 inch. Simmer, covered, for 15-25 minutes until tender but not falling apart.

2. While potatoes are cooking, in a small saucepan heat the cream, butter and goat cheese over moderately low heat. Stir constantly until the butter and cheese are just melted and smooth. Add green onion. Keep warm.

3. Drain the potatoes and garlic. Mash them coarsely with an electric mixer. Beat in the butter and cheese mixture until fluffy and smooth. Season to taste with salt and pepper.

4. Preheat broiler. Transfer potatoes to a 1-quart shallow baking dish. Broil potatoes 4 inches from heat source for 3-5 minutes, or until the top is golden.

Serves 4   *Jan F. Kohl*

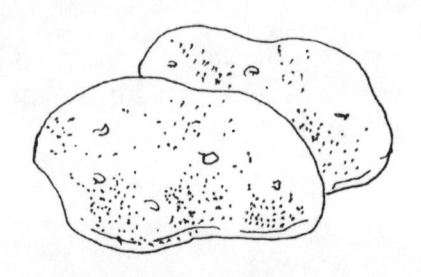

Autumn Side Dishes

PARSNIP PATTIES

1	pound parsnips	2	tablespoons green onion, chopped
3	tablespoons flour		salt and pepper to taste
1	egg		olive oil
1	tablespoon sugar		

1. Peel and cube parsnips. Boil in salted water until tender. Drain and then mash.

2. Combine parsnips with flour, egg, sugar, green onion, salt and pepper.

3. In heavy frying pan, heat enough olive oil to coat bottom.

4. Saute patties until golden brown on each side using 3-4 tablespoons of batter for each. Flatten each patty to about 1/2 inch. Drain well on paper towels.

Makes 12 patties *Sue Taylor*

Note: Parsnip Patties may be prepared ahead for they reheat well in the oven or microwave. They are delicious served as a side dish with meat, or as a main dish accompanied by applesauce and sour cream.

HERBED LENTILS AND RICE

2 2/3	cups chicken broth	1/4	teaspoon dried oregano
3/4	cup dry lentils	1/4	teaspoon dried thyme
3/4	cup onion, chopped	1/4	teaspoon pepper
1/2	cup raw brown rice	1	clove garlic, pressed
1/2	teaspoon dried basil	4	ounces Cheddar cheese, shredded and divided
1/4	teaspoon salt		

1. Preheat oven to 350°.

2. Combine broth, lentils, onion, rice, seasonings and garlic. Stir in half of the cheese. Pour into an ungreased 1 1/2-quart casserole. Bake covered for 1 1/2-2 hours, or until lentils and rice are tender.

3. Sprinkle with remaining cheese. Bake 2-3 minutes, uncovered.

Serves 4-6 *Lisa Herrera*

Autumn Side Dishes

RAMBUNCTIOUS RICE

1 large onion, chopped	1-2 cups cottage cheese
3 tablespoons butter, melted	salt and pepper to taste
4 cups cooked rice	2 1/2 cups Cheddar cheese, grated and divided
2 cups sour cream	1 (4 oz.) can chopped green chilies

1. Preheat oven to 375°.

2. Combine all ingredients (retain 1/2 cup of Cheddar cheese for topping) in a greased 2-quart casserole. Cover.

3. Bake 25 minutes. Sprinkle with remaining cheese and bake 10 minutes uncovered.

Serves 8   *Julie Meredith*

Note: Fast, simple and delicious. A new hit on the potluck circuit!

VEGETABLE RICE PILAF

2 tablespoons olive oil
1 1/2 cups long grain rice, uncooked
1 teaspoon garlic, finely chopped
2 (10 3/4 oz.) cans chicken broth
1/2 teaspoon dried thyme
1/4 teaspoon pepper
2 cups fresh mushrooms, sliced
1 (10 oz.) package frozen peas, thawed
1/4 cup Parmesan cheese, grated
1/4 cup fresh parsley, chopped
2 green onions, sliced

1. Heat oil in Dutch oven. Stir in rice and garlic. Saute over medium heat until rice is browned (4-6 minutes). Add broth slowly. Add thyme and pepper.

2. Continue cooking until mixture comes to a full boil. Reduce heat. Cover and cook 10 minutes. Stir in mushrooms. Cover and cook 5-7 minutes longer until rice is tender. Add peas, parsley, onions and cheese. Heat through.

Serves 6-8   *Vel Ball*

Autumn Entrees

DEVILED ROUND STEAK

2 1/2-3 pounds beef round steak, cut into serving-size pieces	1 large green pepper, sliced
	1 (16 oz.) can tomato sauce
salt and pepper	1 (DR.WT. 4 oz.) can sliced mushrooms
1 egg, beaten	
1 1/2 cups cornflakes, finely crushed	1 cup water
1 tablespoon chili powder	1 clove garlic, pressed
1/4 cup vegetable oil	crushed red pepper flakes to taste
1 large onion, sliced	2 tablespoons dried parsley

1. Trim all fat off meat and pound steak with a meat mallet. Sprinkle with salt and pepper. Dip into egg and then into crushed cornflakes mixed with chili powder.

2. Heat oil in a large, heavy skillet. Brown meat on both sides. Add onion and green pepper. Pour tomato sauce, mushrooms, water, garlic, red pepper flakes and parsley over meat. Cover and simmer 45-60 minutes or until tender. Serve with rice.

Serves 6-8   *Mary Lou Miller*

BAKED CHICKEN ARTICHOKE CASSEROLE

6 chicken breast halves, skinned and boned	2 tablespoons butter, divided
	1 tablespoon flour
1 (17 oz.) can artichoke hearts, drained	1 cup dry white wine
2 cups fresh mushrooms, sliced	1/4 cup dry vermouth
1 clove garlic, minced	salt and pepper to taste
1/2 cup green onion, chopped	fresh whole mushrooms

1. Preheat oven to 350°.

2. Saute chicken breasts in 1 tablespoon butter to brown. Remove to casserole. Saute sliced mushrooms, green onion and garlic. Add to casserole. Trim artichokes as necessary and add to casserole.

3. Melt 1 tablespoon butter and stir in flour. Add wine, vermouth, salt and pepper. Stir and simmer to thicken. Pour over chicken. Bake covered for 45 minutes or until chicken is done. May be made ahead and reheated. Garnish with whole mushrooms.

Serves 4-6   *Roberta Sprowl*

Autumn Entrees

CHICKEN AZTECA

6-8 corn tortillas	1 (DR.WT. 2.5 oz.) can sliced black olives
6 chicken breast halves, cooked and cubed	6 ounces Cheddar cheese, shredded and divided
1 (4 oz.) can chopped green chilies	8 ounces Monterey Jack cheese, sliced
1 small onion, chopped	2 (10 oz.) cans enchilada sauce

1. Preheat oven to 350°.

2. Rinse tortillas in water to soften. Pour 1/2 cup of enchilada sauce on bottom of a greased 9 x 13-inch baking dish. Layer all tortillas in baking dish. Place chicken on top, then layer onion, Cheddar cheese (save 1/2 cup Cheddar cheese to sprinkle on top), black olives and chilies. Top with Monterey Jack cheese.

3. Pour remaining enchilada sauce over all. Sprinkle remaining Cheddar cheese on top. Bake 30-40 minutes.

Serves 6   *Peggy Collyer*

CHILI CHICKEN STEW

6 chicken breast halves, skinned and boned	1 tablespoon chili powder
1 medium onion, chopped	1 tablespoon ground cumin
1 medium green pepper, chopped	1 1/2 teaspoons salt
2 cloves garlic, minced	*Topping:*
1 tablespoon vegetable oil	Cheddar cheese, shredded
2 (14 oz.) cans stewed tomatoes, undrained	sour cream
1 (15 oz.) can pinto beans, drained and chopped	avocado, diced
2/3 cup picante sauce	green onions, sliced

1. Cut chicken into 1-inch pieces. Cook chicken, onion, green pepper and garlic in hot oil in a Dutch oven until lightly browned.

2. Add tomatoes, beans, picante sauce, chili powder, cumin and salt. Cover and simmer 30 minutes.

3. Top each individual serving with cheese, sour cream, avocado and green onions.

Serves 6   *Roberta Sprowl*

Autumn Entrees

CHINESE CHICKEN

- 3 pounds chicken breast, cubed
- 4 ounces slivered almonds
- 1/2 cup celery, chopped
- 1/4 cup onion, chopped
- 1 cup mayonnaise
- 1 tablespoon lemon juice
- 1 (10 3/4 oz.) can cream of mushroom soup
- 1 1/4 cups chicken broth
- 6 ounces chow mein noodles, divided

1. Preheat oven to 350°.

2. Mix together all ingredients with three quarters of the chow mein noodles. Pour into 9 x 13-inch greased baking dish. Top with remaining noodles.

3. Bake 45-60 minutes, or until chicken is completely cooked and juices have evaporated.

Serves 6-8   *Sharon Mennerick*

CHICKEN CACCIATORE

- 4 chicken breast halves, skinned and boned
- 2 tablespoon olive oil
- 1/4 cup fresh mushrooms, sliced
- 1 clove garlic, minced
- 1/2 teaspoon dried oregano
- 1/4 teaspoon ground pepper
- 1 1/2 teaspoons salt
- 2 tablespoons flour
- 2 tablespoons dry sherry or white wine
- 1 (16 oz.) can chopped tomatoes, drained (reserving liquid)

1. Heat olive oil in skillet and brown chicken breasts on both sides. Remove.

2. Add sliced mushrooms to skillet and saute. Add garlic. Return chicken breasts to pan.

3. Make a paste with flour and sherry and then blend in reserved liquid from canned tomatoes. Add to skillet, stirring to blend.

4. Add to skillet chopped tomatoes and seasonings. Cover skillet and simmer 20 minutes or until chicken is tender. Serve with pasta.

Serves 4   *Ron and Jackie Gall*

Autumn Entrees

CHICKEN TETRAZZINI

> 2 pounds spaghetti noodles, uncooked
> 5 pounds chicken meat, cooked and diced
> 1/2 pound butter
> 1 1/2 pounds fresh mushrooms, sliced
> 1/2 cup onion, diced
> 1/2 cup flour
> 1 quart chicken broth
> 2 quarts half-and-half
> 2 pounds assorted cheeses, diced or shredded
> 2 cups white wine
> salt and pepper to taste
> Romano cheese, grated
> dry bread crumbs

1. Cook and drain pasta. Set aside.

2. Preheat oven to 350°.

3. Saute onion and mushrooms in butter. When tender, add flour and stir to make a roux.

4. Add chicken broth. Heat and stir until mixture bubbles. Add chicken, half-and-half, assorted cheese, wine, salt and pepper. Heat thoroughly until cheeses melt.

5. Add chicken mixture to the pasta. Pour into three or four 9 x 13-inch greased baking dishes and sprinkle with grated Romano cheese and bread crumbs.

6. Bake uncovered for 1 hour or until casserole reaches 160° in center.

Serves 25

John Weaver
Inglenook Pantry

Autumn Entrees

BROILED FISH WITH ORANGE MINT SAUCE

- 2 (6 oz.) firm white fish fillets (See Note)
- 1/4 cup fresh orange juice
- 2 tablespoons fresh mint, chopped
- 1 clove garlic, pressed
- 1 teaspoon olive oil
- 1 teaspoon balsamic vinegar
- 1 pinch cayenne pepper
- 1/4 teaspoon salt
- freshly ground pepper to taste

1. Combine orange juice, mint, garlic, vinegar, olive oil and cayenne pepper. Pour over fish. Let marinate 15 minutes.

2. Heat broiler or grill. Remove fish from marinade and sprinkle with salt and pepper.

3. Bring marinade to boil in a small saucepan. Cook at boil 4-5 minutes.

4. Broil or grill fish for about 5 minutes. Baste with the boiled marinade and continue to cook for 2 more minutes.

5. Serve fish with remaining boiled marinade.

Serves 2 *Ron and Jackie Gall*

Note: Any firm white fish such as rockfish, cod, red snapper or halibut may be used. Fresh dill or basil may be substituted for the fresh mint.

Autumn Entrees

CHICKEN NORMANDY

- 6 tablespoons butter or margarine, divided
- 2 large Granny Smith apples, peeled, cored and divided
- 5-6 chicken breast halves, skinned and boned
- flour seasoned with salt and pepper, for dredging
- 1/2 cup Calvados (apple brandy) or applejack brandy
- 1/4 cup chicken broth
- 1/2 cup heavy cream
- fresh parsley

1. Melt 2 tablespoons butter in large skillet. Add half of the apples and saute until barely tender. Reserve for garnish.

2. Wash and pat dry chicken breasts. Dredge in flour mixture. Add 4 more tablespoons of butter and saute chicken breasts. Do not crowd in pan.

3. Add remaining apples and saute until chicken is cooked through. Remove chicken, set aside and keep warm.

4. Add brandy and chicken broth, scraping the bottom of the pan while stirring to reduce slightly. Add cream, stirring constantly as the sauce reduces to a gravy-like consistency. Adjust seasonings.

5. Pour sauce over chicken breasts on serving plate. Garnish with parsley and sauteed apples. Serve immediately.

Serves 4-6   *Penny Newkirk*

Autumn Entrees

ELECTION NIGHT SHRIMP

- 1 (12 oz.) package spinach fettuccine noodles
- 2 pounds fresh shrimp, peeled and deveined
- 1 tablespoon lemon juice
- 1/2 cup white wine
- 2 teaspoons Old Bay Seasoning
- 1/2 teaspoon garlic powder
- 1 (10 3/4 oz.) can cream of mushroom soup
- 1 cup light sour cream
- 1/2 cup light mayonnaise
- 1 teaspoon Dijon mustard
- 2 tablespoons fresh chives, chopped
- 6 tablespoons sharp Cheddar cheese, grated
- 4 tablespoons Parmesan cheese, grated

1. Preheat oven to 350°.

2. Cook noodles as directed on package and place in a greased 9 x 13-inch casserole.

3. Steam shrimp until barely pink but not thoroughly cooked (approximately 1-2 minutes). Place shrimp on top of fettuccine.

4. Combine lemon juice, white wine, Old Bay Seasoning, garlic powder, cream of mushroom soup, sour cream, mayonnaise, mustard and chives. Pour over shrimp to cover. Top with cheeses.

5. Bake covered for 15 minutes. Uncover and bake an additional 15 minutes. Do not overcook or shrimp will toughen.

Serves 8-10

Susan Deuchler
Illinois State Representative

Autumn Entrees

SEAFOOD STUFFED PASTA SHELLS

1	(12 oz.) box large shell pasta
1/2	cup butter
1	small onion, minced
1/4	cup flour
1/4	teaspoon white pepper
	nutmeg, freshly grated
1 1/2	cups milk
1 1/2	cups chicken broth
10	ounces fontinella cheese, shredded and divided
1/4	cup white wine
12	ounces canned or frozen crab
8	ounces fresh or defrosted small shrimp, cooked
3	green onions, thinly sliced
1/2	cup Parmesan cheese, freshly grated

1. Cook pasta shells according to package directions. Rinse in cold water.

2. Preheat oven to 350°.

3. Melt butter in saucepan. Add small onion and saute. Blend in flour, nutmeg and white pepper, stirring constantly. Gradually add milk and chicken broth, stirring until thickened. Add wine and 1 1/2 cups fontinella cheese. Blend. Set aside.

4. Combine crab and shrimp in food processor bowl along with green onions, 1 cup fontinella and the Parmesan cheese. Pulse to blend. Stuff cooked pasta shells. Place shells side by side in a buttered 9 x 13-inch pan to which a small amount of sauce has been added. Spoon sauce over tops. Bake approximately 30 minutes in preheated oven until hot and bubbly.

Serves 8   *Penny Newkirk*

Autumn Entrees

COLORS OF ITALY

24 jumbo shrimp, peeled and deveined	*Pesto sauce:*
4 red peppers	5 cups fresh basil, chopped
4 small Japanese eggplants	1/2 cup fresh parsley, chopped
1/2 pound fresh mushrooms, sliced	3/4 cup Caputo olive oil
1 pound Caputo spaghetti	2 tablespoons garlic, minced
Caputo olive oil	1/2 cup pignoli nuts
Caputo grated Parmesan cheese	1/2 cup Caputo grated Parmesan cheese

1. Pesto Sauce: Add all ingredients to the container of an electric blender and blend, stirring down with a spatula until a smooth paste forms.

2. Peppers: Char peppers over gas flame or in broiler until blackened on all sides. Wrap in paper bag and let stand 10 minutes. Peel, seed and cut peppers into strips. Transfer peppers into large bowl. All cooked vegetables will be put into this large bowl.

3. Eggplants: Cut eggplants into cubes, place on paper towels and salt generously. Let stand 1 hour. Pat dry with paper towels. Pour 1/2 cup of olive oil into medium skillet and saute eggplants until light brown. Place into bowl with red peppers.

4. Spaghetti: Boil water. Add spaghetti. Cook and drain.

5. Mushrooms: While water is boiling for spaghetti saute mushrooms with 2 tablespoons of olive oil. When they are cooked, place mushrooms in vegetable bowl.

6. Shrimp: In large skillet add about 3 tablespoons of olive oil and saute shrimp until pink, not too long or shrimp will become tough.

7. Add all cooked vegetables from large bowl to skillet with shrimp. Cook for 1 minute. Cover and turn off heat. Combine spaghetti, shrimp and vegetables. Toss together with pesto sauce. Top with grated Parmesan cheese.

Serves 4 *Nancy DiMaio*

Note: Nancy won the grand prize with this recipe in the "Caputo Recipe Contest" hosted by Wiscon Corporation, the parent company of Wisconsin Cheese, Inc., manufacturers of Caputo brand products. She donated the entire amount of prize money to Hesed House. (Recipe used with permission.)

Autumn Entrees

SQUASH RATATOUILLE WITH SAUSAGE

4	medium zucchini, cut into 1-inch pieces
2	yellow squash, cut into 1-inch pieces
3-4	carrots, cut diagonally into chunks
8	ounces fresh mushrooms, cut in half if large
2-3	large onions, sliced
3	green peppers, sliced into strips
5	fresh tomatoes, peeled, seeded and coarsely chopped
1/2	cup fresh parsley, chopped
1	teaspoon dried oregano
1	teaspoon dried basil
1	teaspoon dried thyme
	salt and pepper to taste
	flour
	olive oil
3	cloves garlic, minced
1	pound Italian sausage links, cut into bite size chunks

1. Preheat oven to 350°.

2. Coat yellow squash and zucchini with flour. Shake off excess flour. Saute in large skillet with small amount of olive oil. Remove from skillet and saute carrots and mushrooms, onion and peppers until crisp-tender.

3. Layer sauteed vegetables in a baking dish. Add tomatoes, garlic, herbs, salt and pepper. Bake 30-35 minutes.

4. While vegetables bake, saute Italian sausage in skillet. After vegetables have baked for 30 minutes stir in sausage and return to oven for 15-20 minutes longer. Vegetables may be baked 30-35 minutes the day before and browned sausage may be added and warmed through on following day.

Serves 8 *Penny Newkirk*

Note: This recipe is also good with eggplant added.

ITALIAN POTATO CASSEROLE

1 pound bulk Italian sausage, cooked, crumbled and drained	1/2 cup Cheddar cheese, shredded
4 medium russet potatoes, peeled and thinly sliced	1 (15 oz.) can chunky tomato sauce
1 cup onion, sliced	1/2 teaspoon salt
1 1/2 cups green pepper, chopped	freshly ground pepper
1 pound mozzarella cheese, shredded	1 teaspoon dried oregano
	1 teaspoon dried basil
	1 clove garlic, minced

1. Preheat oven to 350°.

2. Grease a 7 x 11-inch baking dish. Combine potatoes, half of the mozzarella cheese and half of the onion in baking dish. Sprinkle with salt, pepper, half of oregano and half of basil.

3. Top potato mixture with cooked sausage, green pepper and remaining onion, oregano, basil and garlic. Pour tomato sauce evenly over all. Bake uncovered for 1 hour.

4. Top with remaining mozzarella cheese and Cheddar cheese. Sprinkle with additional basil. Bake 1/2 hour or until the potatoes are tender.

Serves 4-6

Margaret Kelly

TURKEY MEAT LOAF WITH SUN-DRIED TOMATOES

1 pound ground turkey	1/3 cup milk
1 medium onion, chopped	2 teaspoons fresh rosemary, chopped, or 1/2 teaspoon dried
1 cup fresh bread crumbs	
1 egg, beaten	2 teaspoons fresh oregano, chopped, or 1/2 teaspoon dried
1/2 cup pine nuts, toasted	
12 sun-dried, oil-packed tomatoes, drained and chopped	pepper to taste
	salt, optional

1. Preheat oven to 350°.

2. Combine all ingredients in a large bowl. Mix well.

3. Transfer mixture to an 8 x 4-inch loaf pan. Bake about 50 minutes until loaf pulls away from the side of the pan and the top is golden brown.

Serves 4-6

Jan F. Kohl

Note: This meat loaf is really good cold, or thinly sliced for a picnic.

Autumn Entrees

PRUDENT PIZZA

Crust:
- 1 3/4 teaspoons dry yeast
- 7 ounces water (110°), divided
- 2 teaspoons sugar
- 1/2 teaspoon salt
- 2 1/4 cups all-purpose flour
- 1 tablespoon plus 1 teaspoon olive oil, divided
- cornmeal

Sauce:
- 1 1/2 cups canned chopped tomatoes in puree
- 1 (6 oz.) can tomato paste
- 1 clove garlic, pressed
- 1 teaspoon dried oregano
- 1 teaspoon dried basil

Toppings:
- 1 pound part-skim milk mozzarella cheese, sliced
- 4 ounces fresh mushrooms, sliced
- 1 teaspoon olive oil, divided
- 1 small green pepper, sliced
- 3 green onions, sliced
- 3 tablespoons Parmesan cheese, grated
- 1 teaspoon dried oregano
- 1 teaspoon fennel seed

1. To prepare dough: Dissolve yeast and sugar in 1/4 cup of warm water. Combine flour and salt in food processor. Add dissolved yeast and 1 tablespoon olive oil. With processor running add just enough remaining water so dough forms a ball and cleans the side of bowl. Grease a large bowl with 1 teaspoon olive oil. Add dough and turn to coat. Cover with towel and let dough rise until doubled in size.

2. Combine sauce ingredients and simmer, stirring occasionally until sauce is thick.

3. Saute mushrooms in 1/2 teaspoon olive oil. Do not overcook. Remove from pan and set aside.

4. Preheat oven to 450°.

5. Generously sprinkle cornmeal on a large, lightly oiled pizza pan. On a well-floured surface press the dough out to form a large circle. Transfer dough to prepared pizza pan. Brush 1/2 teaspoon olive oil over dough.

6. Spread sauce evenly over dough. Layer sliced mozzarella, mushrooms, green pepper, green onions, oregano, fennel seed and Parmesan cheese.

7. Bake 20-25 minutes or until crust is golden brown.

Serves 4

Lois Park, R.D.

SWEDISH BISCOTTI

1 cup butter	1/2 teaspoon baking powder
1 cup sugar	2 teaspoons almond extract
2 eggs, separated	1/2 cup slivered almonds, chopped
2 1/4 cups flour	1/4 cup sliced almonds, chopped

1. Preheat oven to 375°.
2. Cream together butter and sugar. Add almond extract, 2 egg yolks and 1 egg white. Add flour and baking powder, then add chopped slivered almonds. Shape into 2 rolls, each 1 inch in diameter. Place on a greased baking sheet.
3. Beat 1 egg white until frothy and brush on top of rolls. Sprinkle with chopped sliced almonds.
4. Bake for 15-20 minutes or until lightly browned and dry in center. Remove from oven and cut into 1/2-inch diagonal pieces. Separate pieces on the cookie sheet.
5. Turn off oven. Return cut pieces to oven until oven has cooled completely and toast is crisp.

Makes 36 pieces   *Anne Nordstrom*

APPLE BARS

1 1/2 cups sugar	3 cups apples, peeled and finely chopped
1 1/2 cups flour	1/2 cup raisins
1 1/2 teaspoons baking soda	1/2 cup nuts, chopped
2 eggs (or egg substitute), beaten	

1. Preheat oven to 350°.
2. Combine sugar, flour and baking soda.
3. Add eggs and chopped apples to dry ingredients. Stir in raisins and nuts.
4. Spread evenly into a greased 9 x 13-inch baking pan.
5. Bake 40-45 minutes.
6. Cool. Dust with powdered sugar just before serving.

Makes 30 bars   *Fran Gustafson*

Autumn Desserts

CRANBERRY CAKE WITH BUTTERED RUM SAUCE

4 tablespoons butter
2 cups sugar
4 cups flour
6 teaspoons baking powder
1 teaspoon salt
2 cups milk
2 teaspoons vanilla
16 ounces fresh cranberries
2 tablespoons orange rind, grated
Buttered Rum Sauce

1. Preheat oven to 350°.

2. Cream together butter and sugar. Combine all dry ingredients. Gradually add dry ingredients to butter mixture.

3. Add milk and vanilla. Blend. Gently fold in cranberries and orange rind. Pour into a greased 9 x 13-inch cake pan. Bake 45-55 minutes or until toothpick inserted into center comes out clean.

4. Serve at room temperature with warm Buttered Rum Sauce *(See Recipe)*.

Makes 18-24 pieces

BUTTERED RUM SAUCE

1 cup half-and-half
2 cups sugar
1 cup butter
1 teaspoon vanilla
2 tablespoons rum or 1 teaspoon rum extract

Heat half-and-half, sugar and butter slowly until sugar dissolves. Add vanilla and rum or rum extract. Bring to a boil. Remove from heat. Serve over Cranberry Cake (See Recipe).

Makes 3 cups   *Paula Brewer*

*Autumn
Desserts*

RAISIN SPICE CAKE

>   2 cups seedless raisins
>   2 cups sugar
>   2 cups cold water
>   3/4 cup margarine
>   3 cups flour
>   1 teaspoon baking powder
>   1 teaspoon ground cloves
>   1 teaspoon ground nutmeg
>   1 tablespoon ground cinnamon
>   1 teaspoon salt
>   1 egg, beaten
>   2 teaspoons baking soda
>   1/2 cup boiling water

1. Grease and flour a 9 x 13-inch pan. Combine raisins, sugar, water and margarine in a large saucepan. Bring mixture just to a boil over medium heat. Remove from heat and allow to cool.

2. Preheat oven to 350°.

3. Combine flour, baking powder, cloves, nutmeg, cinnamon and salt. Mix well.

4. To flour mixture add cooled raisin mixture and egg. Dissolve baking soda in boiling water and add to batter. Mix well. Pour into baking pan.

5. Bake for about 45 minutes until toothpick inserted into center comes out clean. Cool on wire rack.

Serves 15-20   *Susan Mahood*

Note: "*This recipe is from my Great-grandmother Sigsby's private recipe book, handed down for generations.*"

Autumn Desserts

GERMAN APPLE CAKE

    2 cups flour
    2 cups sugar
    2 teaspoons ground cinnamon
    1 teaspoon baking soda
  1/2 teaspoon salt
    2 eggs
    1 cup vegetable oil
    1 teaspoon vanilla
    4 cups apples, peeled, cored and thinly sliced
    1 cup nuts, chopped

Frosting:
    1 (8 oz.) package cream cheese, room temperature
    1 teaspoon vanilla
    3 tablespoons margarine, softened
 1 1/2 cups powdered sugar

1. Preheat oven to 350°.

2. Combine flour, sugar, cinnamon, baking soda and salt.

3. Stir in eggs, oil and vanilla. Mix well with a spoon. Add apples and nuts. Batter will be thick.

4. Bake in a greased and floured 9 x 13-inch baking pan for 45-60 minutes or until toothpick inserted into center comes out clean. Cool.

5. Prepare frosting: Combine cream cheese and margarine. Add vanilla. Beat in powdered sugar. Spread on top of cake.

Makes 20-24 pieces

Tom and Dorothy Milnamow
Pine-Apple Orchard

Autumn Desserts

DECADENT CHOCOLATE PECAN PIE

1	(8-inch) pie crust, unbaked	3	eggs
1/2	cup pecans, chopped	1	teaspoon vanilla
3	tablespoons bourbon	3/4	cup maple syrup
1/4	cup butter, melted	1/4	teaspoon salt
1	cup sugar	1/2	cup semi-sweet chocolate chips

1. Preheat oven to 375°. Soak pecans in bourbon.

2. Beat sugar, butter and eggs until fluffy. Blend sugar mixture with syrup, vanilla and salt. Add chocolate chips.

3. Pour into pastry shell. Sprinkle pecans on top. Bake 45-55 minutes.

Serves 6-8   *Mary Lou Conley*

APPLE RICE DESSERT

1	tablespoon butter or margarine	1 1/4	cups sugar, divided
6	McIntosh apples, peeled, cored and cut into 1/2-inch pieces	3	eggs, well beaten
		1/2	teaspoon ground cinnamon
4	cups cooked white rice, cooled to room temperature	1 3/4	teaspoons vanilla, divided
		1	cup sour cream

1. Preheat oven to 350°.

2. In a warm oven melt butter in a 9 x 13-inch glass baking dish.

3. In a medium bowl combine rice, 3/4 cup sugar, eggs, cinnamon and 1 1/2 teaspoons vanilla. Stir to mix well. Fold in apples. Spread mixture evenly in prepared dish.

4. Bake 25-30 minutes. Cool.

5. To make sauce: In a small bowl combine sour cream, 1/2 cup sugar and 1/4 teaspoon vanilla. Spoon cold sauce on warmed apple rice dessert. Sprinkle with additional cinnamon and serve.

Serves 8-10   *Marilyn Hendry*

Autumn Desserts

GERMAN CHOCOLATE PECAN TORTE

 1 cup butter, softened
 2 cups sugar
 4 egg yolks, beaten
 4 egg whites, beaten stiff
 2 (4 oz.) packages German sweet chocolate
   grated rind of 1 lemon
1 3/4 cups flour
 2 teaspoons baking powder
 1 teaspoon vanilla
 1 cup milk
 8 ounces pecans, coarsely chopped

Glaze:
 1/2 cup semi-sweet chocolate chips, melted
 3-4 tablespoons half-and-half

1. Preheat oven to 350°.

2. Melt German sweet chocolate according to package directions.

3. Cream together butter and sugar. Add egg yolks, German sweet chocolate and lemon rind. Mix well.

4. In a separate bowl combine baking powder and flour. In another bowl combine milk and vanilla. Add flour mixture and milk mixture alternately to the batter. Add chopped pecans. Fold in beaten egg whites.

5. Bake in an ungreased angel food cake pan for 1 hour. Loosen sides and center before releasing onto platter.

6. Blend together semi-sweet melted chocolate and half-and-half to form a glaze. When cake has cooled drizzle with glaze.

Makes 12-16 slices   *Anne Nordstrom*

Autumn Desserts

PUMPKIN TORTE

Crust:
- 1 1/2 cups gingersnaps, crushed
- 1/4 cup butter, melted
- 1/4 cup sugar

Filling:
- 2 (16 oz.) cans pumpkin
- 1 (12 oz.) can evaporated milk
- 4 eggs, lightly beaten
- 1/2 cup brown sugar
- 1 teaspoon ground ginger
- 2 teaspoons ground cinnamon
- 1/4 teaspoon ground cloves
- 1/4 teaspoon ground nutmeg
- 1/2 teaspoon salt
- pecan halves
- whipped cream

1. Preheat oven to 350°.
2. Prepare crust by mixing together gingersnaps, butter and sugar. Press into the bottom of a 9-inch or 10-inch springform pan. Set aside.
3. Combine pumpkin, evaporated milk, brown sugar and eggs. Add remaining filling ingredients except pecan halves and whipped cream. Mix well. Pour filling over prepared crust. Arrange pecan halves on top.
4. Bake for 60-65 minutes or until knife inserted into center of torte comes out clean. Cool. Serve with whipped cream.

Serves 10-12

Carleen Bart
Carol Bushnell

Note: This torte is a wonderful Thanksgiving dessert.

Autumn Desserts

CARROT PUDDING

1 cup carrots, grated
1 cup apples, grated
1 cup raisins
1 cup sugar
3/4 cup butter or margarine
1 teaspoon baking soda
2 cups flour
1 cup pecans, chopped
1 teaspoon ground cinnamon
1 teaspoon ground allspice
Hard Sauce

1. Mix carrots, apples, raisins, sugar and butter or margarine. Sift flour, cinnamon, allspice, and baking soda into carrot mixture. Stir in nuts.

2. Turn into greased tube pan or other deep baking pan, filling two-thirds full. Cover with greased paper and tie with a string.

3. Place on rack in kettle of boiling water. Water should come up halfway around pan. Cover kettle and steam 1 1/2 hours. Keep water boiling gently, adding more hot water as needed. Serve with Hard Sauce *(See Recipe)*.

Serves 12

HARD SAUCE

1 cup unsalted butter, softened
1 cup powdered sugar
1/4 cup brandy or dark rum

1. In medium bowl beat butter until creamy, about 1 minute. Add powdered sugar. Beat until smooth. Add brandy or dark rum.

2. Make up to 2 weeks ahead. Store in covered container in refrigerator. Bring to room temperature and serve with Carrot Pudding *(See Recipe)*.

Makes 1 1/2 cups *Billye Renwick*

Note: "This was often our Thanksgiving or Christmas dessert. A family favorite."

Autumn
Desserts

HUNTERS PUDDING

    4   cups day-old whole wheat bread, cubed
    1   cup raisins
 1/2 cup nuts, chopped
 1/2 cup butter, melted
    1   cup sugar
    1   teaspoon ground cinnamon
 1/2 teaspoon ground cloves
 1/2 teaspoon ground nutmeg
    1   teaspoon baking soda
    1   cup milk
    1   egg
          Orange Sauce

1. Preheat oven to 325°.

2. Combine butter, sugar, spices, baking soda, milk and egg. Stir in bread, raisins and nuts. Pour into greased 7 x 11-inch pan. Bake 60-70 minutes.

3. Serve at room temperature with warm Orange Sauce *(See Recipe)*.

Serves 8

ORANGE SAUCE

    2   tablespoons flour
 1/4 cup sugar
 1/4 teaspoon salt
 1/2 cup corn syrup
    1   cup orange juice
    1   tablespoon butter

In saucepan combine flour, sugar and salt. Add corn syrup and orange juice. Simmer and stir until thickened. Stir in butter. Serve warm over Hunters Pudding *(See Recipe)*.

Makes 1 1/2 cups   Carleen Bart

Note: A wonderful old recipe from Community Hospital in Geneva, Illinois.

Autumn Desserts

BILL'S TIRAMISU

1 pint heavy cream
1 cup sugar
8 large egg yolks,
　at room temperature
3 tablespoons Kahlua
1 pound mascarpone cheese,
　at room temperature
1 1/2 packages saviorde biscuits
1-2 ounces semi-sweet chocolate,
　finely grated

Dipping Sauce:
1 1/2 cups hot water
5 teaspoons instant espresso
1/2 cup Kahlua

1. Prepare zabaglione: Whisk 3 tablespoons of Kahlua, sugar and egg yolks in the top half of a double boiler. Cook over boiling water, whisking constantly until mixture thickens, turns a pale yellow and a candy thermometer registers 170° (about 7 minutes). Remove from heat and set aside.

2. Using an electric mixer, whip cream to form stiff peaks. Whisk mascarpone cheese into zabaglione and then fold whipped cream into the mixture.

3. Make dipping sauce: Combine hot water, espresso and Kahlua to make a dipping sauce. Dunk enough saviorde biscuits in coffee mixture to cover bottom of a trifle dish. Spoon a thick layer of zabaglione mixture over biscuits and cover with a dusting of grated chocolate. Repeat layers, ending with mascarpone mixture dusted with chocolate. Refrigerate for at least 4 hours before serving.

Serves 8　　　　　　　　　　　　　　　　　　　　　　　　　　　　*Jan F. Kohl*

Note: Ladyfingers may be substituted for the saviorde biscuits.

Winter

Table of Contents

Appetizers
Breads
Soups
Salads
Side Dishes
Entrees
Desserts

Winter Appetizers

BLUE CHEESE BALL

- 1 (8 oz.) package regular cream cheese, softened
- 1/4 cup Cheddar cheese spread, softened
- 4 ounces blue cheese, crumbled
- 1/2 cup onion, minced
- 1 tablespoon Worcestershire sauce
- 1/2 cup walnuts, chopped
- 1/4 cup fresh parsley, chopped

1. In a small bowl mix together by hand cream cheese, Cheddar cheese spread, blue cheese, onion and Worcestershire sauce until well blended.
2. Cover and refrigerate until firm.
3. Form cheese into a ball. Roll ball in walnuts and parsley until thoroughly covered.
4. Cover cheese ball and refrigerate. Serve with crackers.

Serves 10   *Ron and Jackie Gall*

Note: More walnuts will be needed to make 2 or 3 small balls.

YUGOSLAVIAN CHEESE SPREAD

- 4 ounces feta cheese
- 1 (8 oz.) package cream cheese, room temperature
- 1/2 cup unsalted butter, room temperature
- 1/2 teaspoon pepper
- 3-4 sprigs fresh rosemary

1. Rinse and drain feta cheese. Beat in mixer or food processor until smooth.
2. Add cream cheese, mix well, and then add butter and pepper.
3. Place into small bowl. Cover and refrigerate until ready to serve. Garnish with fresh rosemary.
4. May be prepared up to 1 month ahead and stored in refrigerator.

Makes 12 servings (1 pound)   *Marilyn Hendry*

Winter
Appetizers

BASIL PARMESAN SPREAD

1/4 cup prepared sun-dried tomato spread
pine nuts
assorted crackers and breads

Pesto Layer:
- 1 cup fresh parsley, packed
- 1 cup fresh basil, packed
- 1 clove garlic
- 6 tablespoons olive oil
- 3/4 cup Parmesan cheese, freshly grated

Cheese Layer:
- 1 (8 oz.) package cream cheese, room temperature
- 4 ounces soft fresh goat cheese, room temperature
- 1 clove garlic

1. Line a 3-cup bowl with plastic wrap, leaving a 4-inch overhang. Set aside.

2. Prepare pesto layer: Wash and dry parsley and basil. Put parsley and basil in food processor and blend with garlic. Add olive oil and Parmesan cheese. Blend.

3. Prepare cheese layer: In clean processor bowl blend cream cheese, goat cheese and garlic until smooth.

4. In prepared bowl layer in this order: One third cheese mixture, a thin layer of pine nuts, a layer of pesto mixture, a thin layer of pine nuts, ending with a layer of tomato spread. Repeat until all of the mixtures are used.

5. Refrigerate several hours or overnight. May be made 3 days ahead.

6. Invert spread onto plate. Remove bowl and plastic wrap.

7. Serve with assorted crackers and breads.

Serves 12

Sally DeCardy
Penny Newkirk

Note: If sun-dried tomato spread is unavailable use oil-packed sun-dried tomatoes. Puree in food processor with 1 tablespoon tomato paste and enough grated Parmesan cheese to thicken mixture to spreading consistency.

Winter Appetizers

TOASTED PARMESAN CRAB CANAPES

- 8 ounces crab meat, minced
- 1 tablespoon fresh parsley, chopped
- 1 teaspoon lemon juice
- 1 teaspoon Worcestershire sauce
- 3 tablespoons Parmesan cheese, grated
- hot sauce to taste
- mayonnaise to moisten
- 30 thin slices of small white onions
- 30 small rounds of bread or cocktail rye bread
- Parmesan cheese, grated

1. Combine crab, parsley, lemon juice, Worcestershire sauce, Parmesan cheese and hot sauce. Add just enough mayonnaise to hold crab mixture together but allow it to remain rather dry.

2. Place an onion slice on each round of bread. Top with crab spread and sprinkle with additional Parmesan cheese.

3. At serving time, place canapes under broiler until tops are nicely browned and bubbly.

Makes 30 canapes

Carol Juntunen
Margaret Kalte

EGGPLANT CAVIAR

- 1 eggplant (about 2 pounds)
- 1 cup onion, finely chopped
- 6 tablespoons olive oil, divided
- 1/2 cup green pepper, finely chopped
- 1 teaspoon garlic, finely chopped
- 2 large ripe tomatoes, peeled, seeded and finely chopped
- 1/2 teaspoon sugar
- 2 teaspoons salt
- freshly ground pepper
- 2-3 tablespoons lemon juice

1. Cook whole eggplant in oven at 425° for 1 hour. Turn once or twice until soft and skin is charred and blistered.

2. Cook onion in 4 tablespoons olive oil until tender and translucent, not brown. Add green pepper and garlic. Cook for a few more minutes.

3. Remove skin from eggplant. Mash until almost a puree. Add eggplant, tomatoes, sugar, salt and pepper to vegetables in skillet with 2 tablespoons olive oil. Simmer about 30 minutes until liquid is reduced. Add lemon juice. Chill before serving with crackers.

Serves 8-12 as appetizer

Donna Nowatzki

Winter Appetizers

SWEET-AND-SOUR MEATBALLS

1	pound ground beef	*Sauce:*	
1/2	pound ground veal	1	(10 oz.) jar apricot or pineapple preserves
2	cups soft bread crumbs		
2	eggs	1/2	cup prepared barbecue sauce
1/2	cup onion, chopped		
1	teaspoon salt		
1/4	teaspoon pepper		

1. Preheat oven to 350°.

2. Combine ground beef, veal, bread crumbs, eggs, onion, salt and pepper. Shape into 1-inch balls and place on jelly roll pan.

3. Bake 30 minutes or until done, turning after 15 minutes.

4. Drain meatballs and place in 2-quart casserole. Mix preserves and barbecue sauce. Pour over meatballs and bake 30 minutes, stirring occasionally.

Makes 6 dozen meatballs　　　　　　　　　　　　　　　　　*Elizabeth Michaelsen*

COCKTAIL MEATBALLS

1	pound ground beef	*Sauce:*	
1/4	teaspoon pepper	2	tablespoons sugar
1/3	cup onion, minced	5	tablespoons Worcestershire sauce
1/2	cup bread crumbs	2	cups catsup or chili sauce
1	teaspoon salt	2/3	cup vinegar
3	tablespoons fresh horseradish		
1	egg		

1. Preheat oven to 350°.

2. Mix all ingredients for meatballs. Shape into 1-inch balls.

3. Combine sauce ingredients, bring to a boil and pour over meatballs. Bake 45 minutes.

4. Refrigerate meatballs. Degrease and reheat for 30 minutes before serving.

Makes 5 dozen　　　　　　　　　　　　　　　　　　　　　*Carol Juntunen*

Note: This is a delicious, spicy meatball.

Winter Appetizers

NEW RED POTATO APPETIZER

  new red potatoes, B size,
   2-3 halves per person
  butter
1 tablespoon fresh dill
1 egg yolk
  fresh chives
  vegetable oil
1/3 cup Creme Fraiche

1. Preheat oven to 400°.

2. Rub new red potatoes with vegetable oil and bake until soft (do not use microwave).

3. Split potatoes in half when cool enough and scoop out flesh. Combine with butter while still warm and mash. Return mashed potatoes to their shells. If potatoes tend to roll make a flattened spot on bottom.

4. Combine Creme Fraiche (See Recipe) with dill and blend in egg yolk. Top potatoes with creme fraiche mixture. Bake until hot and bubbly, approximately 12-20 minutes. Garnish with fresh chives.

CREME FRAICHE

1 cup heavy cream
  (not ultrapasteurized)
1 cup dairy sour cream

1. Whisk heavy cream and sour cream together in a bowl. Cover loosely with plastic wrap and let stand in a warm spot overnight or until thickened.

2. Cover and refrigerate for at least 4 hours. It will continue to thicken. Serve with New Red Potato Appetizer *(See Recipe)*.

Makes 2 cups   *Penny Newkirk*

Note: Potatoes are also great mixed with Boursin Cheese (See Recipe).

Winter Appetizers

ORIENTAL APPETIZER

3/4 cup chicken, cooked and chopped	1/4 teaspoon ground ginger
1/2 cup carrots, shredded	1 garlic clove, minced
1/4 cup water chestnuts, chopped	2 tablespoons red pepper, chopped
3 tablespoons green onion, sliced	Zippy Sweet-and-Sour Sauce
1 tablespoon fresh parsley, minced	assorted crackers
2 teaspoons soy sauce	1 (8 oz.) package cream cheese, softened

1. In medium bowl combine chicken, carrots, water chestnuts, green onion, parsley, soy sauce, ginger, garlic and red pepper. Mix well. Cover and refrigerate 1 hour.

2. In small bowl combine cream cheese and 2-3 tablespoons Zippy Sweet-and-Sour Sauce *(See Recipe)*. Beat until smooth and fluffy. Spread cream cheese mixture over bottom of 10-inch round serving plate.

3. Spoon topping mixture evenly over cream cheese. Drizzle with 1/2 cup Zippy Sweet-and-Sour Sauce. Serve with assorted crackers.

Serves 8-10

ZIPPY SWEET-AND-SOUR SAUCE

1/3 cup sugar
2 tablespoons cornstarch
3/4 cup chicken broth
1/4 cup catsup
1/3 cup red wine vinegar
1 tablespoon Worcestershire sauce

1. In saucepan combine sugar and cornstarch. Stir in remaining ingredients. Cook over medium heat about 5 minutes, or until mixture thickens slightly. Stir frequently.

2. Cool. Store covered in refrigerator. Serve with Oriental Appetizer *(See Recipe)*.

Makes 1 1/2 cups *Marilyn Hendry*

Winter Breads

HONEY GRAIN BREAD

- 2 packages dry yeast
- 2 cups skim or 2% milk, warmed to 110°
- 1/4 cup vegetable oil
- 1/2 cup honey
- 2 eggs, room temperature
- 1 cup regular rolled oats
- 1/2 cup cornmeal
- 1/2 cup wheat germ
- 1 tablespoon salt
- 1 1/2 cups whole wheat flour
- 4-5 cups white bread flour, divided
- 3 tablespoons unsalted sunflower seeds

1. In large mixer bowl combine yeast, warm milk, oil, honey and eggs.

2. Add oats, cornmeal, wheat germ, salt, whole wheat flour and 2 cups of white bread flour. Beat with mixer until dough is stretchy and elastic.

3. Knead in remaining bread flour by hand or use dough hook. Add sunflower seeds.

4. Place dough into a greased bowl, turning over to oil top. Cover with towel and let rise in a warm place until doubled in size. Punch down and press out any air bubbles. Divide in half and shape into 2 round loaves, pulling edges underneath each loaf. Place side by side on 1 large greased cookie sheet or two 9-inch round cake pans. Let rise until doubled, covered with towel.

5. Preheat oven to 350°.

6. Bake 45 minutes or until bottom of loaf sounds hollow when tapped. Remove from pan(s) and cool on rack.

Makes 2 loaves   *Carleen Bart*

Winter Breads

REFRIGERATOR ROLLS

    1   *package dry yeast*
    2   *tablespoons warm water (110°)*
    1   *cup boiling water*
  1/3 *cup sugar*
    2   *tablespoons butter*
    1   *egg, beaten*
    4   *cups flour*
    1   *teaspoon salt*

1. Dissolve yeast in 2 tablespoons warm water.

2. Pour boiling water over sugar and butter. Cool to lukewarm, then add yeast and egg.

3. Combine flour and salt and stir into mixture 1 cup at a time. Knead on a floured work surface, adding more flour as necessary until the dough is smooth and elastic. Place in a greased bowl, turning dough to oil top. Cover with plastic wrap and refrigerate overnight.

4. To prepare rolls, let dough rise at room temperature for 2 hours before shaping.

5. For Parker House rolls: Roll dough to 1/2-inch thickness and cut with biscuit cutter. Fold over and place on greased cookie sheets. Allow rolls to rise about 1 hour, covered, until doubled in size. For cloverleaf rolls: Form dough into small balls, placing 3 in each greased muffin cup. Allow rolls to rise about 1 hour, covered, until doubled in size.

6. Preheat oven to 375°. Bake 15-20 minutes, watching closely, until golden brown. Brush with melted butter.

Makes 2 dozen rolls

Amy Thompson

Winter Breads

SPEEDY ROLLS

1 package dry yeast
1 cup warm water (110°)
3 tablespoons sugar
6 tablespoons vegetable oil
1 teaspoon salt
3 cups flour
1 egg
1/4 cup instant mashed potato flakes

1. Sprinkle water over yeast. Add sugar, oil, salt and egg. Mix well.

2. Stir in flour and potato flakes a little at a time. Turn dough onto a floured board and knead for 1-2 minutes, until smooth.

3. Place dough in a greased bowl, turning to oil top. Cover with plastic wrap and let rise in a warm place until doubled in bulk.

4. Turn dough out onto a floured board and punch down.

5. Roll dough to 3/8-inch thickness. Cut into pie shaped wedges and roll from wide base to point forming a crescent. Place point side down on baking sheet. Cover with plastic wrap and let rise until nearly doubled.

6. Preheat oven to 375°. Bake for 12-15 minutes until golden brown.

Makes 12-16 rolls   *Mary Jane McFee*

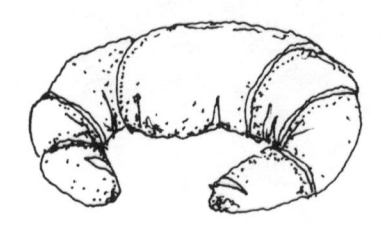

Winter Soups

GARFIELD FARM BEAN SOUP

    2   cups dried beans (See Note)
    5   cups water
    3   cups beef or chicken broth
    1   medium onion, chopped
    2   stalks celery, sliced
    2   ham hocks or 1 ham bone with some meat on it
    1   large carrot, chopped
    1   bay leaf
    1   cup canned tomatoes, chopped
        dash or two hot sauce
        salt and pepper to taste

1. Rinse beans and soak overnight in water. (Or use quick soak method: Cover beans with water, bring to boil and cook 2 minutes covered. Turn off heat and let stand 1-2 hours.)

2. Drain beans and add 5 cups fresh water, ham hocks, tomatoes and broth. Cover and bring to boil. Reduce heat and simmer 2 hours. Remove ham hocks, cut off meat and return it to beans. Discard bones and skin.

3. Add remaining ingredients and simmer 1 hour more. Remove bay leaf. Adjust seasonings.

Serves 8
                                                    Garfield Farm Museum

Note: This recipe was developed to use the old-fashioned varieties of beans grown at Garfield Farm Museum in LaFox, Illinois. They use Dwarf Horticultural beans, Jacob's Cattle beans, Soldier beans, black beans and red lima beans. Any dry bean combination from the grocery store will work. This soup is served at Garfield Farm Fall Harvest Days.

Winter Soups

LENTIL SOUP

2 cups dry lentils
4 cups water
4 cups chicken broth
1 cup onion, finely chopped
1 cup carrots, finely chopped or shredded
1 cup celery, finely chopped
2 tablespoons olive oil
2 bay leaves, cracked
1 tablespoon dried oregano
1 tablespoon dried basil
2 tablespoons dried parsley
2 cloves garlic, finely chopped
1 (28 oz.) can tomatoes, chopped
3 tablespoons wine vinegar
salt and pepper to taste

1. Combine all ingredients in stockpot except tomatoes and vinegar. Bring to a boil and then simmer covered for 1 hour or until lentils are tender.

2. Add tomatoes and vinegar. Simmer for another 30-45 minutes. Add water as needed to achieve desired consistency.

3. Adjust seasonings to taste. Remove bay leaves before serving.

Serves 6-8   *Carol Smith*

Note: Lentil Soup is always better after being refrigerated and reheated the next day.

Winter Soups

MINESTRONE SOUP

1/4	pound dried Great Northern beans
2	tablespoons olive oil
2	tablespoons butter
3/4	cup carrots, chopped
1 1/4	cups celery, chopped
3/4	cup onion, chopped
1	(15 1/2 oz.) can diced tomatoes
2	quarts beef or chicken broth
1	cup potatoes, diced
1	clove garlic, minced
2	tablespoons fresh parsley, chopped
1 1/2	teaspoons dried basil
1/4	teaspoon dried oregano
1/4	pound cooked ham, diced
1/2	package frozen Italian green beans
1/2	pound zucchini, sliced
1/4	cup elbow macaroni
1	cup cabbage, shredded
	Parmesan cheese, freshly grated

1. Wash and soak beans overnight in cold water. Drain. Cook in water to cover until not quite tender. Drain and set aside.

2. Heat oil and butter in skillet. Add carrots, onion and celery. Saute for 5 minutes. Add tomatoes and bring to a boil. Reduce heat and simmer for 10 minutes.

3. Combine broth and potatoes in a soup pot. Bring to a boil and cook just until potatoes are tender. Add the simmering vegetables, Great Northern beans, garlic, parsley, seasonings, ham and green beans. Bring to a boil and simmer for 20 minutes. Add zucchini, macaroni, and cabbage. Simmer 15 minutes or until macaroni is tender. Garnish with grated Parmesan cheese.

Makes 12 cups

Cooking Craft

Winter
Salads

NO-OIL FOUR BEAN SALAD

1 (15 oz.) can kidney beans, with juice
1 (14.5 oz.) can wax beans, drained
1 (15 oz.) can garbanzo beans, drained
2 cups frozen cut green beans
1/2 cup green onion, chopped
1/2 cup green pepper, chopped
1 cup celery, finely sliced
1/2 cup red pepper, chopped
1 cup red wine vinegar
1/2 cup sugar
2 tablespoons Dijon mustard
2-3 teaspoons seasoned salt (or salt free seasoning)
freshly ground pepper to taste

1. Combine vinegar, sugar, mustard, seasoned salt and pepper.

2. Toss vegetables with dressing. Refrigerate overnight before serving.

Serves 10-12 *Carleen Bart*

GERMAN MUSHROOM SALAD

1 pound fresh mushrooms, cleaned and sliced
4 whole sweet pickles, sliced
2 green onions, chopped
1 clove garlic, pressed
4-6 plum tomatoes, cubed
1 (2 oz.) jar diced pimento
1 sprig fresh parsley
1 teaspoon celery seed
1/2 cup vegetable oil
1/4 cup vinegar
2 teaspoons sugar

1. Combine all ingredients. Toss until well coated. Refrigerate until ready to serve.

2. Season with salt and pepper immediately before serving.

Serves 6-8 *Myrtle Abelt*

Winter Salads

BEAN SALAD WITH LIME DRESSING

2 (16 oz.) cans black beans, rinsed and drained	2 tablespoons fresh cilantro, chopped
1/2 teaspoon dried thyme	2 green onions, chopped
1/4 teaspoon fennel seed	1 tablespoon ground cumin
2 garlic cloves, pressed	1/8 teaspoon cayenne pepper
2/3 cup red onion, chopped	1/4 cup olive oil
1/2 cup red bell pepper, chopped	1/2 cup fresh lime juice
2 tablespoons fresh Italian parsley, chopped	salt and pepper to taste
	5-6 ears of corn, blanched and kernels removed from cobs

1. Combine all ingredients. Mix gently until well blended. Chill.
2. Prepare 1 day ahead. Will keep 4 or 5 days in refrigerator.

Serves 8

Jan F. Kohl

Note: One cup of frozen corn may be substituted for fresh corn. This recipe is also good using garbanzo beans instead of black beans, or a mixture of half garbanzo and half black beans.

BROCCOLI SUPREME

2 (10 oz.) packages frozen chopped broccoli, thawed and drained	2 tablespoons onion, chopped
2 eggs	salt and pepper to taste
1 cup mayonnaise	1 1/2 cups Ritz crackers, crushed
1 (10 oz.) can condensed cream of mushroom soup	1 1/2 cups Cheddar cheese, shredded
	2 tablespoons butter, cubed

1. Preheat oven to 350°.
2. Combine eggs, mayonnaise, soup, onion, salt and pepper. Stir in broccoli. Pour into a greased 9 x 13-inch pan. Cover with crushed crackers and cheese. Top with butter.
3. Bake 30-40 minutes.

Serves 6-8

Nola Boyd

Winter Side Dishes

FRIJOLES NEGROS
(Cuban Black Beans)

- 1 pound dried black beans
- 2 large green peppers, chopped and divided
- 10 cups water
- 2/3 cup olive oil
- 1 large onion, chopped
- 4 cloves garlic, pressed
- 1/2 teaspoon freshly ground pepper
- 1/4 teaspoon dried oregano
- 1 bay leaf
- 2 tablespoons sugar
- 2-3 tablespoons balsamic vinegar
- 2 tablespoons dry sherry or white wine
- 2 tablespoons olive oil
- 4 teaspoons salt or to taste

1. Hull and wash dried black beans. In a large pot soak beans and 1 chopped green pepper in water until beans are swollen, about 1 hour.

2. Place pot over moderate heat, bring water to a boil, and simmer until beans are soft, about 45 minutes.

3. While beans are cooking, saute onion and garlic in olive oil. Add 1 chopped green pepper and continue to saute until the vegetables are soft.

4. Remove 1 cup of beans from the pot and mash. Return the mashed beans to the pot along with the sauteed vegetables. Add black pepper, oregano, bay leaf and sugar. Cover and continue to simmer for 1 hour.

5. Add vinegar and sherry and cook slowly for another hour. Add salt to taste. If at this time the beans have too much liquid, uncover and thicken by boiling rapidly. Remove bay leaf.

6. To serve add 2 tablespoons olive oil. Serve with white or yellow (saffron) rice.

Serves 8 *Ron and Jackie Gall*

TEX-MEX CORN

2 cups cream style corn
1 cup prepared biscuit mix
1 egg
1/2 cup milk
2 tablespoons butter, melted
8 ounces Monterey Jack cheese, grated
1 (4 oz.) can chopped green chilies

1. Preheat oven to 350°.

2. Mix together corn, biscuit mix, egg, milk and butter. Place half of mixture in a greased 1 1/2-quart casserole. Place green chilies on top, followed by all but 1/2 cup of grated cheese. Add rest of batter. Sprinkle with remaining 1/2 cup of cheese.

3. Bake 1 hour.

Serves 4-6   *Diane Olsen*

Note: This is a nice side dish to serve with ham.

APPLESAUCE SQUASH

1/4 cup slivered almonds
2 slices soft bread, crumbled
2 tablespoons butter, melted
1 3/4 cups applesauce,
    home style or unsweetened
2 cups acorn or butternut squash,
    cooked and mashed
1/4 cup brown sugar
1/4 cup butter, melted
1/4 teaspoon ground nutmeg
1/2 teaspoon salt
2 eggs, beaten

1. Preheat oven to 375°.

2. Saute bread in 2 tablespoons butter. Add almonds. Set aside.

3. Combine remaining ingredients and pour into a 1 1/2-quart shallow baking dish. Sprinkle bread crumb mixture on top.

4. Bake uncovered for 45 minutes.

Serves 6   *Carol Ludemann*

Winter Side Dishes

BAKED APRICOTS

2 (16 oz.) cans apricots
1/2-3/4 cup brown sugar
1/2 cup cracker crumbs
1/2 cup margarine, melted

1. Preheat oven to 350°.

2. Place 1 can of apricots as first layer in an 8 x 8-inch baking dish. Sprinkle on half of brown sugar and 1/4 cup cracker crumbs. Make another layer of apricots, brown sugar and cracker crumbs.

3. Drizzle melted margarine over all. Bake for 30 minutes. Serve as a condiment with chicken breasts or pork tenderloin.

Serves 6-8   *Roberta Sprowl*

POTATO CASSEROLE

8 medium potatoes
1 bay leaf
1/4 cup butter, melted
1 (15 1/2 oz.) can condensed cream of chicken soup
1 1/2 cups sour cream
salt and pepper to taste
3 green onions, chopped
2 cups sharp Cheddar cheese, grated, and divided
1/2 cup cornflakes, crushed

1. Boil potatoes with skins and bay leaf until barely tender. Remove bay leaf. Cool. Chop potatoes into small pieces.

2. Preheat oven to 350°.

3. In a bowl combine butter, soup, sour cream, salt, pepper, onions and 1 1/2 cups cheese. Pour over potatoes and stir until blended.

4. Pour into greased 2 1/2-quart casserole. Bake 30 minutes, uncovered. Combine remaining 1/2 cup of cheese with cornflake crumbs. Sprinkle over casserole. Bake 10-15 minutes longer.

Serves 8   *Diane Olsen*

Winter Side Dishes

GRATIN OF POTATOES SAVOYARDE

> 3 tablespoons butter or margarine, divided
> 2 cups onion, thinly sliced
> 12-14 medium potatoes, peeled and thinly sliced
>   salt and freshly ground pepper
> 1 cup Swiss cheese, coarsely grated
> 2-3 cups chicken broth as needed

1. Preheat oven to 425°.

2. Saute onion in half of the butter. Grease a large casserole dish and spread with one third of the potatoes. Sprinkle lightly with salt and pepper, then spread one third of the onion, and one third of the cheese. Repeat with 2 more layers, ending with cheese. Dot with the remaining butter and pour in enough chicken broth to come halfway up the potatoes.

3. Place in oven and bake, uncovered, for 50 minutes, until potatoes are tender.

Serves 10-12   *Gisela Kinscheck*

CARROTS MARIETTINA

> 1 (1 lb.) bag baby carrots
> 1/4 cup water (or carrot water)
> 1/2 cup mayonnaise
> 2 tablespoons onion, minced
> 1 1/2 tablespoons horseradish
> 1/2 teaspoon salt
> 1/2 teaspoon pepper
> 1/2 cup fine bread or cracker crumbs
> 1 tablespoon butter, melted
>   paprika

1. Preheat oven to 375°.

2. Cook carrots until tender. Drain, reserving water. Place in a shallow baking dish.

3. Combine water, mayonnaise, onion, horseradish, salt and pepper. Pour over carrots.

4. Combine bread crumbs and butter and spread on top of carrots. Sprinkle with paprika.

5. Bake 15-20 minutes.

Serves 4-6   *S Joanne Vallero, CSJ*

Winter Side Dishes

ALMOND WILD RICE

1 cup golden raisins	6 tablespoons butter, divided
1/2 cup dry sherry	1 cup raw brown rice
1 cup wild rice, uncooked	1 cup slivered almonds
4 cups chicken broth, divided	1/2 cup fresh parsley, chopped
	salt and pepper to taste

1. Simmer raisins and sherry together for 5-10 minutes.
2. Combine wild rice, 2 cups chicken broth and 2 tablespoons butter in the top of a double boiler. Cover and cook for 1 hour.
3. Combine brown rice, 2 cups chicken broth and 2 tablespoons butter in covered saucepan. Cook until rice is tender and water is absorbed, about 50 minutes.
4. Toast almonds in 2 tablespoons of butter until lightly browned.
5. Preheat oven to 325°.
6. Combine all ingredients. Season with salt and pepper to taste. Place in buttered 7 x 11-inch casserole and bake until heated through. Should not be too moist.

Serves 12   *Roberta Sprowl*

Note: *Baking time depends upon whether the dish is prepared in advance and refrigerated or is to be baked at the time of preparation.*

SPICY RICE

1 cup raw converted rice	1/2 teaspoon ground ginger
2 1/2 cups chicken broth	1/4 teaspoon ground turmeric
2 cloves garlic, pressed	1/8 teaspoon cayenne pepper
1 onion, chopped	1/2 cup raisins, optional
1 cup celery, minced	1 cup frozen peas, thawed
1/2 teaspoon salt	1/2 cup green onion, sliced
1 teaspoon ground cumin	

1. In large skillet combine rice with chicken broth, garlic, onion, celery, seasonings and raisins.
2. Bring to a boil. Cover. Simmer 20 minutes or until rice is tender. Stir in peas and green onion. Heat through.

Serves 4-6   *Marilyn Hendry*

*Winter
Entrees*

POT ROAST IN ALE

1 beef chuck roast, 3-4 pounds
2 tablespoons flour
2 tablespoons vegetable oil
1 teaspoon salt
  freshly ground pepper to taste
1 (12 oz.) bottle ale
  water
2 bay leaves
6 medium onions, peeled and sliced
4 carrots, cut into 1-inch pieces
1/2 cup cold water
1/4 cup flour
2 tablespoons catsup

1. Coat roast with flour. In Dutch oven brown in oil on both sides. Season with salt and pepper.

2. Add 1/2 cup ale and bay leaves. Cover tightly and simmer 1 1/2 hours. Add water as needed. Remove bay leaves. Add onions and carrots. Simmer 45 minutes or until vegetables are tender.

3. Remove meat and vegetables to heated platter. Skim fat from meat juices. Add enough ale to juices to make 1 1/2 cups. Whisk cold water with flour until smooth. Stir into juices and add catsup. Cook, stirring, until thickened and bubbly. Season to taste. Simmer 2-3 minutes longer.

4. Serve gravy with meat and vegetables, over potatoes or with noodles.

Serves 4-6   *Linda Wirtz*

Winter Entrees

HESED HOUSE BEEF STEW

> 30 pounds beef stew meat,
>   cut into 1-inch cubes
> 2 gallons beef broth
> 4 pounds celery, chopped
> 4 pounds onions, chopped
> 11 pounds carrots,
>   peeled and cubed
> 12 pounds potatoes,
>   peeled and cubed
> 1 1/2 pounds frozen pearl onions
> 2 1/2 pounds frozen peas
> 1 pound cornstarch
> 2 cups cold water
> salt and pepper to taste

1. Preheat oven to 375°. Brown meat in oven for 45-50 minutes. Turn once or twice for even searing.

2. In a very large stockpot, on top of stove, combine meat and beef broth. Simmer until tender, approximately 2 hours. Remove meat from broth and keep warm. Be careful not to overcook meat.

3. Place carrots, celery, potatoes and onions in broth. Simmer until barely tender. Return meat to the cooked vegetables and heat. If needed, add more liquid to completely cover the ingredients.

4. Dissolve cornstarch in water. Add to stew to thicken. Add frozen peas and pearl onions to mixture and simmer 15 minutes, stirring frequently. Season to taste.

Serves about 100

Ed Troy
St. Rita of Cascia

Note: *This is a favorite recipe at Hesed House PADS.*

Winter Entrees

BAKED CHICKEN IN WHITE WINE AND CAPER SAUCE

6	chicken breast halves, skinned and boned	1/2	teaspoon garlic powder
1/2	cup flour	1 1/2	cups dry white wine
1	teaspoon paprika	2	tablespoons margarine
1/2	teaspoon pepper	2	tablespoons capers, drained

1. Preheat oven to 450°. Grease baking dish.
2. Combine flour with paprika, pepper and garlic powder in a plastic bag. Shake chicken in flour mixture to coat evenly. Arrange chicken in greased baking dish and pour wine over the top. Dot with margarine and sprinkle with capers. Cover with foil.
3. Bake 20 minutes, then reduce heat to 325° and bake until chicken is cooked thoroughly, about 50 minutes.

Serves 4-6   *Mary Lou Conley*

Note: Serve over wild rice or spinach fettuccini noodles.

FRENCH ONION PIE

	pastry for one 9-inch pie crust, baked to light golden brown	1 1/2	cups milk
1	(3 1/3 oz.) can French fried onions, divided	1/2	cup sharp Cheddar cheese, shredded
		1	cup Swiss cheese, shredded
3	eggs	1/2	teaspoon salt
			dash cayenne pepper

1. Preheat oven to 325°.
2. Fill pie crust with 1 1/2 cups French fried onions.
3. Beat eggs slightly, blend in milk and Cheddar cheese, salt and cayenne. Pour over onions in pie crust. Sprinkle the Swiss cheese over all.
4. Bake for 45 minutes. Sprinkle remaining 1/2 cup of onions on pie. Bake 5-10 minutes more until golden brown.
5. Let stand at room temperature for 5 minutes. Cut in wedges to serve.

Serves 6   *Marilyn Hendry*

Winter Entrees

CARIBBEAN CHICKEN

  4 chicken breast halves, skinned and boned
  2 tablespoons butter or margarine
1/2 cup onion, chopped
1/2 cup celery, sliced
  1 cup rice, uncooked
1/3 cup raisins
  2 cups apple juice
  1 teaspoon salt
1/2 cup pecan pieces
1-2 teaspoons curry powder
1/2 cup apple brandy or white wine
  1 tablespoon flour
1/2 cup chicken broth
1/2 cup half-and-half
  1 Granny Smith apple, peeled and chopped
  2 tablespoons butter

1. Melt butter or margarine in saucepan. Stir in curry powder, onion and celery. Saute. Add rice, raisins, apple juice and salt. Bring to a boil. Cover and simmer 15 minutes or until rice is tender. Stir in pecans. Place in greased 9 x 13-inch baking dish.

2. Preheat oven to 325°.

3. Saute chicken breasts until lightly browned. Remove from pan and place on rice. In the same pan saute apple in butter. Place apple on top of chicken.

4. Deglaze the pan with apple brandy or white wine. Add flour and cook, stirring over low heat for 1-2 minutes. Add chicken broth and half-and-half. Continue stirring until the sauce thickens. Pour over chicken and rice.

5. Bake 25 minutes.

Serves 4   *Penny Newkirk*

Winter Entrees

MEDITERRANEAN CHICKEN

1 large clove garlic, pressed	1/4 teaspoon pepper
1 cup onion, chopped	1 bay leaf
1 1/2 cups green pepper, chopped	1 tablespoon dried marjoram
1 1/2 cups mushrooms, sliced	1 tablespoon dried parsley
1 tablespoon olive oil	1/2 teaspoon ground allspice
1 1/2 pounds chicken breasts, skinned and boned	1/4 cup white wine
1 (28 oz.) can crushed tomatoes	2-4 tablespoons tomato paste
1 (28 oz.) can whole peeled tomatoes, cut in quarters	

1. Saute garlic, onion, green pepper and mushrooms in olive oil.

2. Add all the other ingredients except wine and tomato paste. Simmer until chicken is cooked thoroughly, about 45 minutes.

3. Remove chicken and pull it apart with 2 forks to shred into bite size pieces. Return chicken to sauce along with wine and tomato paste and cook to desired consistency. Simmer to heat before serving.

4. Serve over pasta or rice.

Serves 6   *Carleen Bart*

SALMON PIE

2 tablespoons margarine or butter, melted	3 tablespoons lemon juice
1/2 cup milk	2 teaspoons onion, finely chopped
4 slices bread, torn into pieces	1 teaspoon salt
1 (15 1/2 oz.) can salmon, drained and flaked	1/2 teaspoon pepper
2 eggs, separated	paprika

1. Preheat oven to 350°.

2. Mix butter, milk and bread. Stir in salmon, egg yolks, lemon juice, onion, salt and pepper.

3. Beat egg whites until stiff. Fold into salmon mixture. Pour into greased 8-inch pie plate. Sprinkle with paprika.

4. Bake uncovered 50-60 minutes.

Serves 4   *Mary Stasek*

Note: To microwave, use glass pie plate, but do not grease. Microwave on high 5-7 minutes until top is dry.

Winter Entrees

APRICOT-STUFFED PORK TENDERLOIN

 4 boneless pork tenderloins (1 1/2 lbs. each)
 1 (6 oz.) package long grain and wild rice mix
 1/2 cup boiling water
 1/2 cup dried apricots, chopped
 2 green onions, finely chopped
 1/2 cup fresh mushrooms, chopped
 2 tablespoons butter
 3 tablespoons pecans, chopped
 1/4 cup green pepper, chopped
 1 tablespoon fresh parsley, chopped
 1/8 teaspoon salt
 1/8 teaspoon pepper
  dash of red pepper
  dash of garlic powder
 4 slices bacon
  apricot halves
  fresh parsley

1. Pour boiling water over dried apricots and let stand for 20 minutes to soften. Drain.

2. Saute green onions, mushrooms, and green pepper in butter until tender. Add rice, softened apricots, pecans, chopped parsley and seasonings.

3. Cut a lengthwise slit on top of each tenderloin, being careful not to cut through the bottom and sides. Spoon half of the stuffing into the opening of 1 tenderloin. Place cut side of second tenderloin over stuffing. Tie tenderloins together securely with string and place on a rack in a roasting pan. Top with 2 slices of bacon. Repeat procedure with remaining tenderloins. Refrigerate until ready to bake.

4. Preheat oven to 325°.

5. Cover tenderloins with aluminum foil. Bake for 1 1/2-2 hours or until meat thermometer registers 170°. Remove foil the last 30-40 minutes. Remove from oven. Let stand 5 minutes before removing string. Slice carefully. Serve garnished with apricot halves and parsley.

Serves 8-10   *Carlleen Pierson*

Winter Entrees

SALMON WITH TOMATO BASIL VINAIGRETTE

4 (6 oz.) salmon fillets
4 tablespoons olive oil
1/4 cup balsamic vinegar
1/4 cup fresh basil, finely chopped
2 tablespoons fresh lemon juice
2 tablespoons honey
2 teaspoons Dijon mustard
salt and freshly ground pepper
2 whole tomatoes, peeled, seeded and chopped
fresh basil leaves

1. In a small bowl mix 4 tablespoons of the oil with vinegar, chopped basil, lemon juice, honey, mustard, salt and pepper.

2. Transfer half of the mixture to a flat pan and add salmon fillets. Seal tightly and marinate in the refrigerator for a minimum of 2 hours.

3. Stir the chopped tomatoes into the remaining marinade. Cover and refrigerate.

4. Preheat oven to 450°. Remove fish from marinade and set fish aside. Pour marinade into a large oiled oven-proof skillet. Heat on stove. When marinade is hot add salmon seasoned with salt and pepper, skin side down. Cook for 2 minutes.

5. Transfer skillet to the preheated oven and bake for 5 minutes, just until fish is cooked.

6. In a small saucepan warm the refrigerated tomato marinade. Spoon tomato marinade over the salmon and garnish with basil leaves.

Serves 4 *Ron and Jackie Gall*

Winter Entrees

CASSOULET

3 cups canned white Northern beans, drained	**Bouquet Garni:**
1 pound Italian sausages	2-3 sprigs fresh parsley
1 cup white wine	1 large bay leaf, cracked
1 cup water	10 whole peppercorns
4-5 strips bacon, cut crosswise	6 whole allspice
1 large onion, cubed	2 teaspoons dried thyme
2-3 carrots, peeled and cut into 1-inch chunks	8 whole cloves
1-1 1/2 pounds roasted pork loin, cubed	
2 chicken breast halves, cooked and cubed	
3 cloves garlic, minced	
1 tablespoon tomato paste	
1 tablespoon chili sauce	
2 tablespoons brandy	

1. Preheat oven to 350°.

2. Pierce sausages with a fork and saute in a small amount of grease until browned. Add white wine and water to sausages. Simmer until heated through. Drain and reserve steaming broth. Cut sausages into thirds.

3. Place beans in large earthenware casserole. Place sausages over beans. Add bacon, onion, carrots, pork loin and chicken.

4. Place all garni spices in a cheesecloth bag and put in casserole.

5. Add enough reserved steaming broth from sausages to just cover casserole ingredients. Add garlic, chili sauce and tomato paste for color. Add brandy and stir.

6. Bake, covered, 30 minutes. Uncover and bake an additional 45 minutes or until vegetables are soft and casserole is bubbly and hot. Remove bouquet garni. Let stand, covered, 10-15 minutes before serving.

Serves 6-8   *Penny Newkirk*

Note: The traditional duck or goose may be used in place of chicken.

Winter Entrees

MRS. V'S LASAGNA

  olive oil
2 pounds ground beef
2 medium onions, chopped
2 small cloves garlic, minced
1/2 teaspoon dried oregano
2 bay leaves
2 tablespoons fresh parsley, minced
1 (28 oz.) can whole tomatoes, chopped
7 cups tomato puree
2 pounds ricotta cheese
4 eggs, beaten
1 pound brick or mozzarella cheese, thinly sliced
  Parmesan cheese, grated
1 (16 oz.) package lasagna noodles, cooked
  salt and pepper to taste

1. In Dutch oven, saute onions and ground beef in olive oil. Cook thoroughly, but do not brown. Drain.
2. Add garlic, tomatoes, tomato puree and herbs. Simmer 30-40 minutes. Add salt and pepper to taste. Remove bay leaves.
3. While sauce is cooking, blend ricotta with eggs. Beat well. Set aside.
4. Preheat oven to 350°.
5. Cover bottoms of two 9 x 13-inch baking dishes with sauce, then noodles. Spread ricotta mixture in a very thin layer on the noodles. Then place a layer of sliced cheese on the ricotta layer. Repeat layers. End with a layer of noodles and then sauce. Top with Parmesan cheese. Use extra baking pans if necessary. Pans may be frozen at this point. Thaw in refrigerator before baking or increase baking time.
6. Bake 45-60 minutes (60-90 minutes if frozen).

Makes two 9 x 13-inch pans   S Joanne Vallero, CSJ

Note: *"This is an old family favorite for celebrations and get togethers."*

Winter Entrees

PAELLA HONDURAS

1 cup converted rice, uncooked
2 cups chicken broth, divided
1/4 cup margarine
1 pound chicken breasts, skinned, boned and sliced
2 bay leaves
1/2 pound Polish sausage, diced small
1/2 cup onion, sliced
1/2 cup green pepper, sliced
1/2 cup celery, diced
1/4 cup corn, fresh or frozen
1 cup green peas, fresh or frozen
1/4 cup raisins
1 1/2 teaspoons curry powder
1/2 teaspoon garlic powder
1/2 teaspoon pepper
salt to taste
1/2 teaspoon turmeric

1. Boil chicken in broth with bay leaves until tender. Remove bay leaves and reserve broth to boil rice.

2. In a medium frying pan, melt margarine. Do not burn. Add sausage and rice. Fry until slightly brown, stirring often. Add onion, green pepper and celery to the rice and sausage. Saute for about 10 minutes.

3. Add 1 cup chicken broth and cook 10 minutes more. Add corn, peas, raisins, chicken, 1 cup of chicken broth and spices. Cook 15 minutes, covered, over low heat until the rice is tender and fluffy.

Serves 4-6   *Suyapa Anderson*

Note: Suyapa Americanized this recipe from her native Honduras.

Winter Entrees

MIDWEST PASTIES

Filling:
- 1 pound lean, tender beef, cooked
- 1 clove garlic, pressed
- 2 stalks celery, finely chopped
- 1 medium onion, finely chopped
- 2 large carrots, medium diced
- 1 large turnip, medium diced
- 2 medium potatoes, medium diced
- 1/2-1 cup beef broth and meat juices
- salt and pepper to taste
- 3/4 teaspoon dried thyme
- 1/4 cup fresh parsley, chopped

Crust:
- 3 cups all-purpose flour
- 3/4 teaspoon salt
- 1 1/4 cups solid vegetable shortening
- 7-9 tablespoons cold water

1. Prepare filling: Pulse meat in food processor to coarsely chop. Save juice. Combine meat with garlic, celery, onion, carrots, turnip and potatoes. Moisten with broth. Add salt, pepper, thyme and parsley.

2. Prepare crust: In medium bowl stir together flour and salt. With pastry blender or 2 knives cut shortening into flour to resemble coarse crumbs. Sprinkle cold water, a tablespoon at a time, into flour mixture. Mix lightly with fork after each addition until dough is just moist enough to hold together. Shape dough into 6 pieces. On lightly floured surface with floured rolling pin, roll 1 piece of dough into a 9-inch circle, about 1/8-inch thick. Use a plate to trim circle.

3. Preheat oven to 400°. Place 1 cup of filling, drained, on pastry circle. Brush edges with water. Fold crust over filling to form a half circle, and seal edges by pressing with fork. Repeat to make 6 pasties. Transfer carefully to jelly roll pans covered with greased aluminum foil. Cut vent holes in top of each pastie and brush with milk. Bake 1 hour or until golden brown.

4. Serve with chili sauce and/or horseradish sauce (mix horseradish cream sauce with sour cream to taste).

Serves 4-6 *Carleen Bart*

Winter Desserts

CHOCO-CHERRY BARS

1/2 cup butter, melted
2 ounces unsweetened chocolate, melted
1 cup sugar
2 eggs
1/2 teaspoon baking powder
1/2 cup flour
1/2 cup nuts
1/3 cup maraschino cherries, chopped
1 teaspoon vanilla

Frosting:
1 tablespoon butter, melted
1 cup powdered sugar
1 ounce unsweetened chocolate, melted
1 teaspoon vanilla
1-2 tablespoons maraschino cherry juice

1. Preheat oven to 350°.

2. Combine butter, chocolate and sugar. Add eggs, baking powder and flour. Stir in vanilla, cherries and nuts. Pour into greased 8-inch square pan. Bake for 30-35 minutes. Cool.

3. Prepare frosting: Combine butter, chocolate, powdered sugar, vanilla and cherry juice. Frost bars.

Makes 16 bars

Dorothy Gunter
Elgin High School
Clumsy Chef
Restaurant and Catering Co.

Winter Desserts

GERMAN SWEET CHOCOLATE COOKIES

1/2 cup margarine	1 teaspoon vanilla
1/2 cup butter	2 cups flour
1/2 cup brown sugar	1 teaspoon baking soda
1/2 cup white sugar	1/4 teaspoon salt
1 egg	1 (4 oz.) bar German sweet chocolate, grated

1. Cream butter and margarine together. Add sugars and beat until well blended. Add egg and vanilla. Stir in remaining ingredients until well blended.
2. Divide dough in half and roll into logs about 1 1/2 inches in diameter. Wrap in plastic wrap and refrigerate until chilled.
3. Preheat oven to 350°. Slice cookies 1/4-inch thick. Bake 10 minutes on ungreased cookie sheet until lightly browned on the bottom. Remove immediately to cool.

Makes 2 dozen cookies *Carleen Bart*

Note: "This cookie was my Aunt Vivian's specialty. A family favorite."

MILK CHOCOLATE BALLS

1 (15 1/2 oz.) box graham cracker crumbs, divided	2 squares (1 oz. each) unsweetened chocolate
2 cups sugar	2 cups mini marshmallows
1 (5 oz.) can evaporated milk	1/2 cup nuts

1. In heavy saucepan combine sugar, evaporated milk, and chocolate. Heat just until past melting point. Cool to lukewarm.
2. Add 2 1/4 cups graham cracker crumbs, marshmallows, and nuts.
3. Shape into small balls, 1 inch in diameter. Roll in remaining graham cracker crumbs.
4. Store in an airtight container.

Makes 4 dozen balls *Roberta Mitchell*

Note: "I remember making these at Christmas with my Grandpa Campbell." A great Christmas treat for children of all ages.

Winter Desserts

GINGERSNAPS

3/4 cup butter	2 teaspoons baking soda
1 cup brown sugar	1/2 teaspoon ground cloves
1 egg	1 teaspoon ground ginger
4 tablespoons molasses	1 teaspoon ground cinnamon
1/4 teaspoon salt	granulated sugar
2 1/4 cups flour	

1. Cream butter and brown sugar. Add egg and molasses. Beat in dry ingredients except granulated sugar. Chill dough a few hours.

2. Preheat oven to 350°. Roll dough by hand into small balls. Roll in granulated sugar. To flatten, press with bottom of glass that has been dipped in water.

3. Bake on ungreased cookie sheet 10 minutes or until lightly browned. Remove to rack to cool. Serve with Homemade Lemon Curd *(See Recipe)*.

Makes 3 dozen cookies   Carol Erickson

HOMEMADE LEMON CURD

3 eggs, slightly beaten	3/4 cup sugar
1/2 cup fresh lemon juice	1/4 cup butter, cut in cubes
zest of one lemon	

1. In top part of double boiler combine eggs and lemon juice. Whisk and blend. Add lemon zest, sugar and butter.

2. Cook over hot water until thickened, whisking constantly.

3. Test doneness by inserting a metal spoon into curd. It should coat the back of the spoon like a custard. Cool and refrigerate until ready to use.

Serving suggestions:

1. A filling for tarts or between cake layers.

2. A sauce to serve over pound cake.

3. A dip for cookies, especially Gingersnaps *(See Recipe)*.

Makes approximately 1 cup   Penny Newkirk

Winter Desserts

CREAM CHEESE COOKIES

3/4	cup butter	*Frosting:*	
1/2	cup sugar	2	cups powdered sugar
1	(3 oz.) package cream cheese	1/4	cup butter
1/4	teaspoon salt	1	teaspoon vanilla
1	teaspoon vanilla	1-2	tablespoons half-and-half as needed
1 1/2	cups flour, sifted		nuts, chopped

1. Cream together butter, cream cheese, sugar and salt. Add vanilla, then flour. Mix well. Chill 1 hour.
2. Preheat oven to 350°.
3. Roll into 3/4-inch balls. Press flat with fork dipped in powdered sugar.
4. Bake on ungreased cookie sheet for 10-12 minutes until edges are lightly browned. Cool.
5. For frosting: Beat butter and vanilla into powdered sugar. Whip in as much half-and-half as needed. Spread on cooled cookies. Sprinkle with nuts.

Makes 5 dozen cookies   Roberta Mitchell

HOLIDAY CHOCOLATE PARFAIT

1 1/2	envelopes unflavored gelatin	1/4	teaspoon salt
1/2	cup cold water	1	cup sugar
1	cup egg substitute	2	teaspoons vanilla
2	cups heavy cream, whipped	1 1/2	cups chocolate cookie crumbs

1. Soak gelatin in water, then melt in a double boiler over boiling water.
2. Whip cream and set aside.
3. Blend egg substitute, salt, sugar and vanilla. Mix well. Slowly add gelatin, beating constantly. Fold in whipped cream.
4. Alternate layers of mixture with layers of cookie crumbs, beginning and ending with crumbs. Dessert may be prepared in a 7 x 11-inch baking dish, a 9-inch springform pan or individual parfait glasses. Chill in refrigerator until ready to serve.

Serves 8-12   Carol Hundley

Note: "This is a Hundley holiday favorite, served for over 50 years."

Winter Desserts

PFEFFERNUSSE COOKIES

1 1/2	cups light corn syrup
2 1/4	cups sugar
1/2	cup margarine
1/2	cup milk
1/2	cup sour cream
1	teaspoon lemon rind, grated
2	teaspoons baking powder
8	cups flour
1	teaspoon ground anise seed
1	teaspoon ground cinnamon
1/4	teaspoon ground cloves
1	teaspoon ground nutmeg
1/2	teaspoon ground mace
1	teaspoon ground ginger
1	teaspoon ground cardamom

1. Cream margarine and sugar. Add syrup, milk, sour cream and lemon rind. Mix well.

2. Add baking powder, spices and flour. Mix well. Dough will be very stiff. Cover and refrigerate overnight.

3. Roll dough into logs 1/2-inch in diameter using a small amount of flour on the counter. Place in container with wax paper between layers. Freeze logs.

4. Preheat oven to 325°.

5. Cut frozen dough into 1/8-inch thick pieces using kitchen shears. Place directly onto a greased cookie sheet. Bake 15 minutes until evenly browned to a medium light color. Remove cookies from sheet and place on a lint free towel to cool and dry, separating any that have touched during baking.

6. Cool thoroughly, then store in tightly covered jar or can. Pfeffernusse seem to mellow and get better with age.

Fills a 1 gallon storage jar *Fern Bart*

Note: Parchment paper works well instead of greasing the baking sheets. Pfeffernusse make a great Christmas gift.

ITALIAN LEMON KNOTS

1 1/2 cups sugar
7 eggs
1 cup solid vegetable shortening
5 cups flour
5 teaspoons baking powder
1 teaspoon lemon extract

Frosting:
3 cups powdered sugar
milk
lemon juice
yellow food coloring or
    sprinkles to decorate, optional

1. Preheat oven to 350°.

2. Cream together sugar, eggs and shortening. Add flour, baking powder and lemon extract. Mix well. Chill. This dough will stay soft.

3. On a lightly floured surface roll a portion of the dough into a coil 1/2-inch in diameter by 5 inches long. Overlap the ends of the dough into a loop on a parchment paper lined baking sheet. Repeat process until all dough has been used. Bake 10-12 minutes until lightly browned around the edges. Cool completely on a rack.

4. Prepare frosting: Mix powdered sugar with enough milk and lemon juice until smooth and fairly thin. Frost cookies.

Makes 5-6 dozen cookies   *Martha Rioux*

Winter Desserts

WALDORF RED CAKE

    1/2 cup butter
1 1/2 cups sugar
    2 eggs
    1 (1 oz.) bottle red food coloring
    1 teaspoon vanilla
    2 teaspoons vinegar
    2 tablespoons cocoa
    1 teaspoon salt
    1 cup buttermilk
2 1/4 cups cake flour
    1 teaspoon baking soda

Cooked Frosting:
    5 tablespoons flour
    1 cup milk
    1 cup sugar
    1 teaspoon vanilla
    1 cup butter

1. Preheat oven to 350°. Grease and flour two 8-inch cake pans.

2. Cream butter and sugar to the consistency of whipped cream. Add eggs and blend. Add coloring and cocoa. Add buttermilk and salt alternately with flour. Always start and end with flour. Add vanilla. Mix vinegar and baking soda. It will foam. Add to cake batter and beat. Pour batter into prepared cake pans. Bake 30-35 minutes. Cool.

3. Prepare frosting: Cook flour and milk until thick. Cool. Cream sugar, butter and vanilla until fluffy. Blend in cold milk and flour mixture (which should have the consistency of cold oatmeal). Beat at high speed, for 5 minutes, scraping down sides of bowl. Final mixture should look like whipped cream.

4. Split each cake into 2 layers. Frost between layers and on top of cake.

Serves 12   *Carol Erickson*

Note: Be ready to spend a little time on this cake. The results are well worth it.

Winter
Desserts

BAKLAVA

1 1/2	cups walnuts, ground medium fine	*Syrup:*	
1	teaspoon ground cinnamon	1	cup water
1/4	teaspoon ground nutmeg	1	cup sugar
1	cup clarified butter, melted	1	small stick cinnamon
1	pound filo dough,	10	whole cloves
	room temperature for 1 hour	1	tablespoon lemon juice
		1/2	cup honey

1. Combine walnuts, cinnamon and nutmeg. Set aside.
2. Prepare syrup: In a saucepan combine sugar, water, cinnamon stick, cloves and lemon juice. Boil 8 minutes and remove from heat. Discard cinnamon stick and cloves. Add honey and set aside.
3. Use an 8 1/2 x 1 1/2-inch disposable round foil cake pan. Have the filo opened and the sheets lying flat. Take the foil pan and lay it face down on the filo. With a sharp knife, cut all around and to the bottom of the filo 1/2-inch larger than the pan. Place the pan far enough over on the sheet so 2 may be cut from the same sheet of filo. Put 1 pile over the other and cover with plastic wrap to keep from drying out. Set aside.
4. Brush pan with butter. Lay 1 sheet of filo in pan. Brush with butter. Repeat until there are 10 sheets in pan.
5. Spread 1 full tablespoon of nut mixture evenly over filo. Cover with another sheet. Press with hand to adhere nuts and remove all bubbles. Brush with butter and use another tablespoon of nuts. Repeat until all nuts are used and then finish by topping with about 10 sheets of filo, brushing each and pressing into place. With scissors, cut the filo all around the edges of pan and with the help of a pointed knife tuck in the cut edges of the filo, making a smooth top and edging.
6. With a sharp thin knife cut in strips 1 1/2-inches wide to the bottom of the pan. Turn the pan around and score into diamond shapes to the bottom of the pan, making 24 whole pieces plus corners.
7. Preheat oven to 350°.
8. Drizzle lightly with cold water and bake for 60 minutes. Lower heat to 250° and bake for another 30 minutes.
9. Remove from oven. Let stand for 15 minutes to cool slightly. With a tablespoon pour warm syrup over each piece and between the rows. May be frozen ahead and thawed.

Makes 24 pieces   *Patty Dritsas*

Winter Desserts

FRUIT CAKE DELUXE

- 1 pound pitted dates
- 1 cup glazed pineapple, cut in wedges
- 1 cup glazed whole cherries
- 1 cup walnut halves
- 1 cup pecan halves
- 1 cup whole Brazil nuts
- 3/4 cup flour
- 3/4 cup brown sugar or white sugar
- 3/4 teaspoon baking powder
- 1/2 teaspoon salt
- 3 eggs
- 1 teaspoon vanilla

1. Preheat oven to 300°. Prepare four 3½ x 6-inch pans. Spray with nonstick cooking spray and line with parchment paper. Spray parchment paper.

2. Place all whole fruits and nuts in a large bowl.

3. Sift flour, sugar, baking powder and salt over the fruits and nuts. Mix until they are well coated.

4. Beat eggs and add vanilla. Pour over fruit, nut and flour mixture. Mix well. There will be very little batter. Press firmly into prepared pans.

5. Bake 60-75 minutes until firm. Let stand until cool. Remove from pans and remove paper. Wrap in foil or plastic wrap. Store in refrigerator or freezer.

Makes 4 small loaves   *Fran Gustafson*

Note: "This recipe has been in my family for 3 generations."

INDEX

A

Almond Wild Rice 142
Antipasto, Grilled 57
Antipasto Tortorice 42
Appetizer
    Antipasto Tortorice 42
    Basil Parmesan 125
    Blue Cheese Ball 124
    Boursin Cheese 44
    Cheese-Stuffed Surullitos 84
    Cocktail Meatballs 127
    Eggplant Caviar 126
    Goat Cheese Spread with Tomatoes . . 17
    Marinated Shrimp 17
    Mexican Dip 84
    New Red Potato Appetizer 128
    Oriental 129
    Pita Chips 85
    Salsa Cilantro 43
    Sangria 45
    Shrimp Cheese 19
    Spinach and Cheese 18
    Strawberry Rumba 43
    Sweet-and-Sour Meatballs 127
    Tangy Apricot 19
    Toasted Parmesan Crab Canapes . . . 126
    Yugoslavian Cheese Spread 124
Apple
    Bars 113
    Brie Soup 88
    Cake, German 116
    Rhubarb Squares 35
    Rice Dessert 117
    Torte, Bavarian 10
Applesauce Squash 139
Apricot(s)
    Appetizer, Tangy 19
    Baked 140
    Stuffed Pork Tenderloin 148
Artichoke
    and Hearts of Palm Salad 49
    Chicken Casserole, Baked 101
Asparagus
    Casserole 25
    Salad, Fresh 21
    Soup 20
    Timbales 24

B

Baked Apricots 140
Baked Beans, Bart's 59
Baked Chicken Artichoke Casserole . . . 101
Baked Chicken in White Wine
    and Caper Sauce 145
Baklava 161
Banana Pecan Bread 11
Barbecued Beef 63
Bars
    Apple 113
    Choco-Cherry 154
    Rhubarb Apple 35
    Rhubarb Custard Squares 34
    Symphony Tea 75
Bart's Baked Beans 59
Basil Parmesan Spread 125
Bavarian Apple Torte 10
Bean(s)
    and Easter Ham Soup 20
    and Rice Salsa, Black 68
    Bart's Baked 59
    Cuban Black 138
    Salad, No-Oil Four 136
    Salad with Lime Dressing 137
    Soup, Garfield Farm 133
Beaumonde Bread 46
Beef
    Barbecued 63
    Chinese Pepper Steak 27
    Cocktail Meatballs 127
    Deviled Round Steak 101
    Irish Corned 28
    London Broil 61
    Midwest Pasties 153
    Mrs. V's Lasagna 151
    Polynesian Steak Kebabs 63
    Pot Roast in Ale 143
    Stew, Hesed House 144
    Sweet-and-Sour Meatballs 127
Belgian Malted Waffles 7
Beverage, Sangria 45
Bill's Tiramisu 122
Biscotti, Swedish 113
Biscuits
    Busy Day 86
    Cornmeal Sour Cream 86

Index

Black Bean
    and Feta Salad 49
    and Rice Salsa 68
    Hummus 85
Blue Cheese
    Ball 124
    Dressing 22
Blueberry
    Jam, Spiced 6
    Syrup 8
Boursin Cheese 44
Bran Muffins, Green Meadows' 14
Bread
    Banana Pecan 11
    Bavarian Apple Torte 10
    Beaumonde 46
    Busy Day Biscuits 86
    Cappuccino Chip Muffins 12
    Cornmeal Sour Cream Biscuits 86
    Cranberry 87
    Cream Cheese Coffee Cake 16
    Grandma Goldie's Coffee Cake 15
    Green Meadows' Bran Muffins 14
    Herbed Garlic 46
    Honey Grain 130
    Refrigerator Rolls 131
    Rhubarb 14
    Speedy Rolls 132
    Strawberry 11
    Sweet Irish Cream 15
    Sweet Nut Braid Coffee Cake 13
Brie Apple Soup 88
Broccoli
    Rice, Grecian 26
    Supreme 137
Broiled Fish with Orange Mint Sauce . . 105
Busy Day Biscuits 86
Buttered Rum Sauce 114

C

Cabbage, Red, Sweet-and-Sour 96
Cake
    Cranberry with
        Buttered Rum Sauce 114
    Emma's Schaum Torte 81
    Fruit Deluxe 162
    German Apple 116
    German Chocolate Pecan Torte . . . 118
    Hummingbird 39
    Light-As-Air Sponge 77
    Picnic Chocolate 76
    Pineapple Upside-Down 40
    Polish Easter Torte 38
    Pumpkin Torte 119
    Raisin Spice 115
    Rhubarb Crunch 36
    Waldorf Red 160
Candy, Chocolate Deadlies 36
Cappuccino Chip Muffins 12
Caribbean Chicken 146
Carrot(s)
    Harvest 95
    Lyonnaise 94
    Mariettina 141
    Pudding 120
Cashew Salad with Poppy Seed Dressing . . 92
Cassoulet 150
Celery Soup, Cream of 89
Cheddar Potato AuGratin 26
Cheese
    and Spinach Appetizers 18
    Blintzes 3
    Shrimp Appetizers 19
    Stuffed Surullitos 84
Cheesecake, Deli-Style 77
Chicken
    Artichoke Casserole, Baked 101
    Azteca 102
    Breasts, Mandarin 30
    Breasts, Marinated 64
    Cacciatore 103
    Caribbean 146
    Cassoulet 150
    Chinese 103
    Corn Soup, Pennsylvania Dutch 90
    Country Captain 30
    Hawaiian 32
    in White Wine and
        Caper Sauce, Baked 145
    Mediterranean 147
    Normandy 106
    Oriental Appetizer 129
    Paella Honduras 152
    Salad, Curried 53
    Salad, Hot 5
    Stew, Chili 102
    Tetrazzini 104
    Thai-Style Grilled 64
    Veldene 29
Chili
    Chicken Stew 102
    Quiche 29
Chinese Chicken 103
Chinese Pepper Steak 27

Index

Choco-Cherry Bars 154
Chocolate
    Balls, Milk 155
    Cookies, German Sweet 155
    Deadlies 36
    Parfait, Holiday 157
    Peanut Butter Pie 81
Cinnamon Syrup 8
Cocktail Meatballs 127
Coffee Cake
    Cream Cheese 16
    Grandma Goldie's 15
    Sweet Nut Braid 13
Coleslaw Vinaigrette 65
Colors of Italy 109
Cookie
    Cream Cheese 157
    Eleanor's Oatmeals 37
    German Sweet Chocolate 155
    Gingersnaps 156
    Greatest Sugar 37
    Italian Lemon Knots 159
    Milk Chocolate Balls 155
    Pfeffernusse 158
Corn
    Chicken Soup, Pennsylvania Dutch . . 90
    Pudding 94
    Tex-Mex 139
Corned Beef, Irish 28
Cornmeal Sour Cream Biscuits 86
Country Captain 30
Cranberry
    Bread 87
    Cake with Buttered Rum Sauce . . . 114
    Relish 93
Cream Cheese
    Coffee Cake 16
    Cookies 157
Cream of Celery Soup with Stilton 89
Creme Fraiche 128
Curried
    Chicken Salad 53
    Mayonnaise 53

D

Danish Cream Garlic Potatoes 96
Danish Potato Salad 50
Decadent Chocolate Pecan Pie 117
Deli-Style Cheesecake 77
Deviled Round Steak 101
Dip
    Black Bean Hummus 85
    Mexican 84
Duluth Poppy Seed Dressing 22

E

Easter Ham and Bean Soup 20
Egg Casserole, Ranchero 4
Eggplant
    Caviar 126
    Verdura 60
Eleanor's Oatmeals 37
Election Night Shrimp 107
Emma's Schaum Torte 81

F

French Onion Pie 145
French Roasted Potatoes 97
French Toast For Brunch 5
Fresh Asparagus Salad 21
Fresh Herb Pasta Sauce 73
Fresh Strawberry Syrup 9
Fresh Strawberry-Lemon Pie 78
Fresh Tomato Herb Soup 47
Frijoles Negros (Cuban Black Beans) . . 138
Frittata, Vegetable 2
Fruit Cake Deluxe 162
Fruit Salad Dressing 51

G

Garfield Farm Bean Soup 133
Gazpacho
    Jan's 48
    Pasta Toss 54
German Apple Cake 116
German Chocolate Pecan Torte 118
German Mushroom Salad 136
German Sweet Chocolate Cookies 155
Gingersnaps 156
Goat Cheese
    Mashed Potatoes 98
    Spread with Tomatoes 17
Golden Parmesan Potatoes 58
Grandma Goldie's Coffee Cake 15
Gratin of Potatoes Savoyarde 141
Greatest Sugar Cookie 37
Grecian Broccoli Rice 26
Green Meadows' Bran Muffins 14
Grilled Antipasto 57
Grilled Swordfish
    with Tomato Herb Salsa 70

H

Ham and Bean Soup 20
Hard Sauce 120
Harvest Carrots 95
Hawaiian Chicken 32

Index

Herbed Garlic Bread 46
Herbed Lentils and Rice 99
Hesed House Beef Stew 144
Holiday Chocolate Parfait 157
Homemade Lemon Curd 156
Honey Grain Bread 130
Hot Chicken Salad 5
Hummingbird Cake 39
Hunters Pudding 121

I
Irish Corned Beef 28
Italian Lemon Knots 159
Italian Potato Casserole 111
Italian Sausage
    Potato Casserole 111
    Squash Ratatouille with 110
Italian Tomato and Onion Salad 52

J
Jam, Spiced Blueberry 6
Jan's Gazpacho 48
John's Rack of Lamb 31

K
Key Lime Pie 80
Kugel with Applesauce 4

L
Lamb
    John's Rack 31
    Kebabs and Balsamic Vinegar 33
Lasagna, Mrs. V's 151
Layered Spinach Salad 52
Lemon Curd, Homemade 156
Lemonade Pie 78
Lentil
    and Rice, Herbed 99
    Soup 134
Light-As-Air Sponge Cake 77
London Broil 61

M
Mandarin Chicken Breasts 30
Mango Salsa 71
Margarita Pie 79
Marinated Chicken Breasts 64
Marinated Shrimp 17
Mayonnaise, Curried 53
Meatballs
    Cocktail 127
    Sweet-and-Sour 127

Mediterranean Chicken 147
Mediterranean Vegetable Stew 62
Mexican Dip 84
Midwest Pasties 153
Milk Chocolate Balls 155
Minestrone Soup 135
Mixed Greens with
    Creamy Raspberry Dressing 23
Mrs. V's Lasagna 151
Muffins
    Cappuccino Chip 12
    Green Meadows' Bran 14
Mushroom(s)
    Salad, German 136
    Scalloped 95

N
New England Clam Chowder 91
New Red Potato Appetizer 128
No-Oil Four Bean Salad 136

O
Oatmeals, Eleanor's 37
Onion(s)
    and Tomato Salad, Italian 52
    Classic Casserole 25
    Pie, French 145
    Sautéed 61
Orange Sauce 121
Oriental Appetizer 129
Oriental Spinach Salad 21

P
Paella Honduras 152
Palm, Hearts of and Artichoke Salad 49
Paris Potato Salad 50
Parsnip Patties 99
Pasta
    and Shrimp with Caper-Basil
        Vinaigrette 66
    and Vegetables 73
    Chicken Tetrazzini 104
    Kugel with Applesauce 4
    Salad, Rotini 56
    Sauce, Fresh Herb 73
    Shell, Seafood Stuffed 108
    Toss, Gazpacho 54
Pasties, Midwest 153
Pennsylvania Dutch Chicken Corn Soup .. 90
Pesto Sauce for Pasta 74
Pfeffernusse Cookies 158
Picnic Chocolate Cake 76

Index

Pie
    Chocolate Peanut Butter 81
    Decadent Chocolate Pecan 117
    Fresh Strawberry-Lemon 78
    Key Lime 80
    Lemonade Pie 78
    Margarita 79
    Salmon 147
    Turtle 80
Pineapple
    Salad 92
    Upside-Down Cake 40
Pita Chips 85
Pitakey Sandwiches 71
Pizza, Prudent 112
Polish Easter Torte 38
Polynesian Steak Kebabs 63
Poppy Seed Dressing, Duluth 22
Pork
    Cassoulet 150
    in Red Chili Sauce 66
    Sandwiches with Coleslaw, Taylor's . . 65
    Sausage Strata 2
    Spinach Terrine 31
    Tenderloin, Apricot-Stuffed 148
Pot Roast in Ale 143
Potato(es)
    and Chive Saute, Sugar Snap Pea . . . 57
    Casserole 140
    Casserole, Italian 111
    Cheddar AuGratin 26
    Danish Cream Garlic 96
    French Roasted 97
    Goat Cheese Mashed 98
    Golden Parmesan 58
    New Red Appetizer 128
    Salad, Danish 50
    Salad, Paris 50
    Savoyarde, Gratin of 141
    Sherried Sweet 97
Prudent Pizza 112
Pudding
    Carrot 120
    Hunters 121
Pumpkin
    Soup, Tailgate 91
    Torte 119
    Waffles 7

Q

Quiche
    Chili 29
    Zucchini 72

R

Rainbow Sherbet Macaroon 82
Raisin Spice Cake 115
Rambunctious Rice 100
Ranchero Egg Casserole 4
Raspberry Dressing,
    Creamy with Mixed Greens 23
Reddened Shrimp 67
Refrigerator Rolls 131
Relish, Cranberry 93
Rhubarb
    Apple Squares 35
    Bread 14
    Crunch Cake 36
    Custard Squares 34
Rice
    Almond Wild 142
    and Lentils, Herbed 99
    Apple Dessert 117
    Grecian Broccoli 26
    Pilaf, Vegetable 100
    Rambunctious 100
    Salsa, Black Bean and 68
    Spicy 142
Rotini Pasta Salad 56
Rum Fruit Salad 51

S

Salad
    Artichoke and Hearts of Palm 49
    Bean with Lime Dressing 139
    Black Bean and Feta 49
    Broccoli Supreme 137
    Cashew with Poppy Seed Dressing . . 92
    Curried Chicken 53
    Danish Potato 50
    Fresh Asparagus 21
    Gazpacho Pasta Toss 54
    German Mushroom 136
    Hot Chicken 5
    Italian Tomato and Onion 52
    Layered Spinach 52
    No-Oil Four Bean 136
    Oriental Spinach 21
    Paris Potato 50
    Pineapple 92
    Rotini Pasta 56
    Rum Fruit 51
    Spinach 54
    Tabbouleh 55
    Ultimate 93

Index

Salad Dressing
    Blue Cheese 22
    Coleslaw Vinaigrette 65
    Creamy Raspberry 23
    Duluth Poppy Seed 22
    Fruit 51
Salmon
    Pie 145
    with Tomato Basil Vinaigrette 149
Salsa
    Cilantro 43
    Mango 71
    Tomato Herb 70
Sandwiches
    Pitakey 71
    with Coleslaw, Taylor's Pork 65
Sangria 45
Sauce
    Buttered Rum 114
    Creme Fraiche 128
    for Pasta, Pesto 74
    Fresh Herb Pasta 73
    Hard 120
    Orange 121
    Zippy Sweet-and-Sour 129
Sausage Strata 2
Sauteed Onions 61
Scalloped Mushrooms 95
Scalloped Tomatoes 58
Sea Bass, Teriyaki 62
Seafood
    Broiled Fish with
        Orange Mint Sauce 105
    Colors of Italy 109
    Election Night 107
    Marinated Shrimp 17
    New England Clam Chowder 91
    Salmon Pie 147
    Salmon with
        Tomato Basil Vinaigrette 149
    Shrimp Brunch Casserole 3
    Stuffed Pasta Shells 108
    Teriyaki Sea Bass 62
    Toasted Parmesan Crab Canapes . . . 126
Sherbet Macaroon, Sherbet 82
Sherried Sweet Potatoes 97
Shrimp
    and Pasta with Caper-Basil
        Vinaigrette 66
    Brunch Casserole 3
    Cheese Appetizers 19
    Colors of Italy 109

Election Night 107
Marinated 17
Reddened 67
Side Dishes
    Almond Wild Rice 142
    Applesauce Squash 139
    Asparagus Timbales 24
    Asparagus Casserole 25
    Baked Apricots 140
    Bart's Baked Beans 59
    Broccoli Supreme 137
    Carrots Lyonnaise 94
    Carrots Mariettina 141
    Cheddar Potato AuGratin 26
    Corn Pudding 94
    Cranberry Relish 93
    Cuban Black Beans 138
    Danish Cream Garlic Potatoes 96
    Eggplant Verdura 60
    French Roasted Potatoes 97
    Goat Cheese Mashed Potatoes 98
    Golden Parmesan Potatoes 58
    Gratin of Potatoes Savoyarde 141
    Grecian Broccoli Rice 26
    Grilled Antipasto 57
    Harvest Carrots 95
    Herbed Lentils and Rice 99
    Parsnip Patties 99
    Potato Casserole 140
    Rambunctious Rice 100
    Scalloped Tomatoes 58
    Scalloped Mushrooms 95
    Sherried Sweet Potatoes 97
    Spicy Rice 142
    Sugar Snap Pea,
        Potato and Chive Saute 57
    Sweet-and-Sour Red Cabbage 96
    Tex-Mex Corn 139
    Vegetable Rice Pilaf 100
    Vidalia Onion Classic Casserole . . . 25
Soup
    Apple Brie 88
    Asparagus 20
    Chili Chicken Stew 102
    Cream of Celery with Stilton 89
    Easter Ham and Bean 20
    Fresh Tomato Herb 47
    Garfield Farm Bean 133
    Jan's Gazpacho 48
    Lentil 134
    Mediterranean Vegetable Stew 62
    Minestrone 135

Index

New England Clam Chowder 91
Pennsylvania Dutch Chicken Corn .. 90
Sweet Potato 89
Tailgate Pumpkin 91
Zucchini 47
Spaetzle (German Dumplings) 90
Speedy Rolls 132
Spiced Blueberry Jam 6
Spicy Rice 142
Spinach
   and Cheese Appetizers 18
   Salad 54
   Salad, Layered 52
   Salad, Oriental 21
   Tart, Summer 69
   Terrine 31
Spread
   Basil Parmesan 125
   Blue Cheese Ball 124
   Boursin Cheese 44
   Goat Cheese with Tomatoes 17
   Yugoslavian Cheese 124
Squash
   Applesauce 139
   Ratatouille with Sausage 110
Stew
   Hesed House Beef 144
   Mediterranean Vegetable 62
Strawberry
   Bread 11
   Rumba 43
   Syrup, Fresh 9
Sugar Snap Pea, Potato and Chive Saute .. 57
Summer Spinach Tart 69
Summer Tomato Sauce with Linguine ... 72
Swedish Biscotti 113
Sweet Irish Cream Bread 15
Sweet Nut Braid Coffee Cake 13
Sweet Potato Soup 89
Sweet-and-Sour Meatballs 127
Sweet-and-Sour Red Cabbage 96
Swordfish, Grilled with
   Tomato Herb Salsa 70
Symphony Tea Bars 75
Syrup
   Blueberry 8
   Cinnamon 8
   Fresh Strawberry 9

T
Tabbouleh Salad 55
Tailgate Pumpkin Soup 91
Tangy Apricot Appetizer 19
Taylor's Pork Sandwiches with Coleslaw .. 65
Tex-Mex Corn 139
Thai-Style Grilled Chicken 64
Timbales, Asparagus 24
Tiramisu, Bill's 122
Toasted Parmesan Crab Canapes 126
Tomato(es)
   and Onion Salad, Italian 52
   Herb Salsa 70
   Herb Soup, Fresh 47
   Sauce with Linguine, Summer 72
   Scalloped 58
Turkey Meat Loaf
   with Sun-Dried Tomatoes 111
Turtle Pie 80

U
Ultimate Salad 93

V
Vegetable Frittata 2
Vegetable Rice Pilaf 100
Vegetables and Pasta 73
Vegetarian Entrees
   Chili Quiche 29
   French Onion Pie 145
   Pasta and Vegetables 73
   Prudent Pizza 112
   Summer Spinach Tart 69
   Summer Tomato Sauce
      with Linguine 72
   Zucchini Quiche 72
Vidalia Onion Classic Casserole 25

W
Waffles
   Belgian Malted 7
   Pumpkin 7
Waldorf Red Cake 160

Y
Yugoslavian Cheese Spread 124

Z
Zippy Sweet-and-Sour Sauce 129
Zucchini
   Quiche 72
   Soup 47

Seasoning the Fox Valley

$15.00 each
(Add $3.75 shipping and handling for 1st book
and $1.00 for each additional copy)

Make checks payable to:
PADS Cookbook

Mail to:
Hesed House PADS Cookbook
659 S. River Street
Aurora, Illinois 60506